THE y

OF FLEET STREET

... AND ME

A Memoir

Alix Kirsta

First published in 2024

ISBN: 978-1-0686146-0-6

To my beloved husband the late John Zieger

By the same author

Skin Deep

Stress Survival

Victims

Deadlier Than The Male

Manhattan Murder Mystery

Island of the Damned

Contents

1

The Man Next Door

THE STREET DOOR slammed and I knew instantly something was wrong. Home after school on a rain-sodden winter afternoon, I stepped into deafening silence. The lobby of the block was deserted and a growing unease gripped my throat, the first warning of a panic attack. I repeatedly jabbed the lift button, willing myself upstairs in the safety of my flat. But instead of the reassuring whirr of the mechanism easing into action, violent banging and a frenzied rattling of metal rent the air, suggesting a lunatic on the rampage. Heart pounding, I headed for the familiarity of the crowded street when a barrage of expletives echoed down the staircase, followed seconds later by a plaintive groan.

With a gasp of relief, I turned back and began climbing the stairs.

Our stately 19th Century lift had broken down, clearly trapping some unfortunate soul inside. It was stuck halfway between the second and third floor landing where I peered through the window of the shaft door. Several feet below, facing the control panel, stood a short, middle-aged man in a fedora and raincoat. Under one arm he clutched a gaping briefcase, wrestling with bundles of newspapers and documents that threatened to tip onto his feet. With his free hand he manically shook the iron gate, then stabbed the red alarm button with mounting rage.

"Oh, for flaming hell's sake. Shhh… shit and bugger! Fuck!!"

I tapped the glass. "Can I help?"

His head swung around and he shot me a furious glance. Blue-grey eyes, a high forehead crumpled with anger. He was in big trouble and in no mood for niceties, still less an embarrassing confrontation with a twelve-year-old schoolgirl.

Looking daggers at me, his expression switched instantly to naked embarrassment.

"Out of action again. Third time this year," he muttered, tight-lipped. "And the fu… I'm frightfully sorry… please forgive my language… the *blasted* porter apparently can't hear the alarm."

I offered to fetch help: the porter's lodge was in one of the blocks further along the street. Still shamefaced at being caught out by a child, he thanked me with evident relief, explaining he was running twenty minutes late for a conference at the other end of town.

"I would be enormously grateful, if it isn't too much trouble. Are you visiting?"

I explained that my mother and I had moved into a top flat two months earlier.

"Oh, you're the new neighbours, flat N on the top floor? Mine's M, next door."

He cracked a sheepish grin.

"I'm your neighbour, Harold Keeble. Welcome to Portman Mansions, Baker Street's temple to modern technology!"

* * *

Until that afternoon, I had no idea who lived next door to us. My mother and I had only recently moved into the Victorian mansion complex in Chiltern Street, a quiet backwater behind the junction of Baker Street and Marylebone Road. We were out for most of the day: my mother worked long hours at the theatrical costumier's business she founded shortly before the sudden death of my father two years earlier, when he and I were shopping in the West End. Years later, I realised that witnessing his fatal heart attack had programmed my unconscious mind to enter panic mode at moments of sudden stress, as before I discovered Harold Keeble in the lift.

I wasn't surprised that we hadn't met any neighbours. We moved to Marylebone from Chelsea, and I missed the bohemian jollity of my childhood home, with its non-stop street theatre: French onion sellers on bicycles, rag and bone merchants, cane chair weavers, cutlery sharpeners, raffish locals parading along the King's Road. I still remembered, aged seven, watching the lamplighter on a tall ladder lighting the old street lamps each evening outside my father's studio in our flat in Jubilee Place. By comparison, Marylebone seemed dull and uninspiring.

To me, training to be a professional dancer, attending ballet classes every day in the West End after school, Portman Mansions was the epitome of restrained gentility. You could spend week after week without seeing anyone come in or out of the building except for tradesmen, or one of the porters doing his rounds or delivering the mail. Living five storeys up on the top floor meant we were even more cut off from tenants on other floors and I suspected there might be no other children in the building. I was the new kid on the block. Sure enough, I soon discovered I was indeed the only kid. But, having briefly met Harold Keeble and played a part in his release from captivity, for which he and his wife later thanked my mother profusely, I was curious to know more about him. Little did I guess how long it would take to satisfy that curiosity.

We saw little of the Keebles. The couple had no children and maintained an elusive presence, though traces of high living occasionally drifted in their wake. The dying notes of French perfume or cigar smoke in the hall; a tinkle of expensive jewellery; the click of high heels and swish of fur as Mrs Keeble, tall and glamorous, swept into the flat.

In contrast, the cast of characters orbiting the Keeble's home became a source of fascination. From time to time, a tall, lantern-jawed man in a chauffeur's cap and a lugubrious expression would stand outside their front door, waiting to escort the couple downstairs with their luggage into a waiting Daimler. On some mornings around 8.30, a middle-aged woman in a tweed suit carrying a briefcase, whom I took to be a secretary, was ushered indoors.

What especially caught my eye was the variety of English and foreign newspapers, magazines, books, sheaves of foolscap and mock newspapers stuck together on pieces of cardboard that piled up outside their door, or were delivered by various dishevelled-looking men in ill-fitting suits. They always seemed to be in a hurry, impatiently ringing the doorbell, handing over the stashes and dashing downstairs rather than wait for the lift. With the Keeble's flat a hub of behind-the-scenes activity, this constant coming and going served only to heighten the mystery surrounding the couple.

Their housekeeper, Queenie, arrived most mornings as I was going off to school and stayed until late afternoon. Eventually, we discovered from our cleaning lady, who got chatting to Queenie, that Harold Keeble was a Fleet Street editor working on the highest selling newspaper at the time, the *Daily Express*.

Despite all the peripheral activity, like T.S.Eliot's mystery cat Macavity, little was seen of Harold Keeble in those days. After my first encounter with him in the broken lift, sightings were rare and fleeting and I sensed something cloak and dagger about his activities. His front door sometimes was left slightly ajar and I became aware of a figure skulking in the shadows; presumably he delayed his exit to avoid having to talk to me, my mother or my Viennese grandmother who spoke no English – bar the occasional "Gootten Aa-fternun" – and he obviously thought better of trying to squeeze into the rickety lift with us. If we accidentally bumped into one another, he mumbled a perfunctory greeting but had little to say to a schoolgirl lugging a huge tote bag to dance class.

They were an odd couple. Mary Keeble, an elegant brunette with the glossy sophistication of a *Vogue* model and her husband, who reminded me of a cross between Orson Welles and a more handsome James Cagney. Short, stocky with a trace of pugnaciousness, he had a fleshy face, retroussé nose, and a full upper lip that unfurled into a captivating smile. Usually in a dark suit and black raincoat, he projected a certain louche glamour and could have stepped out of Damon Runyon's Broadway stories of 1940s New York and its *demi-monde* of gamblers, gangsters and chorus girls.

Suddenly one spring, an eerie silence descended on our landing. The normally busy lift, with its juddering hydraulics and clattering gates, audible even inside our flat, fell silent. The Keeble's chauffeur and the parade of *Daily Express* minions vanished. When all the next door windows remained dark, we realised we were alone on the top floor. A month later, we heard that the couple had set out for Bournemouth for the out-of-town premiere of a new musical called *The World of Paul Slickey,* based on the fictitious *Daily Express* gossip columnist William Hickey. On the way, the Keeble's Daimler was involved in a massive road accident, which killed Mary Keeble and the chauffeur instantly and left her husband with severe multiple injuries. For almost a year we saw and heard nothing from next door and learnt later that Harold Keeble had spent seven months in hospital recovering from extensive internal injuries and multiple fractures, including a shattered leg that left him with a permanent limp.

* * *

The next door flat remained unoccupied for so long that we wondered whether Harold Keeble had moved out following the appalling tragedy. But when he finally returned to Portman Mansions, to our astonishment a second Mrs Keeble soon appeared centre stage, whom he married in early 1961. Blonde, very young and pretty, without Mary's sophistication, Susan

Keeble seemed scatty and vague, ringing our bell unexpectedly at times asking distractedly if we could let her have some sugar or milk because she had "suddenly" run out.

It didn't take a genius to work out that this second marriage was heading for the rocks. While Harold and Mary's domestic life had seemed to sail smoothly on untroubled waters, his partnership with Susan took off in a force ten gale. Doors slammed; voices were raised; lights stayed on throughout the night, followed, more ominously, by the flat being plunged into darkness for nights on end. You could almost smell the cordite. Years later, I heard a story from someone whose father, Lionel Green, was a close friend of the Keebles. It summed up the imbroglio playing out next door.

"My father got a phone call one Saturday lunchtime from Harold, who begged him to come over to the flat immediately because he needed help. Susan had gone berserk, locked herself into one of the rooms and was smashing everything up inside. He drove over right away and for the next hour, he and Harold tried talking to Susan and finally persuaded her to unlock the door. Eventually, she calmed down and came out and after a while my father knew he had helped Harold as much as he could and so left Portman Mansions and went home."

The episode ended on a delicious note of farce.

"About ten minutes after my father left, Harold's doorbell rang. When he answered the intercom, a man's voice enquired, 'Do you want any knives sharpening?' Convinced my father had returned to play a joke on him, Harold shouted, 'Fuck off, Lionel!' In fact it really *was* a knife sharpener ringing around the neighbourhood offering his services."

As his marriage unravelled, Harold again became an infrequent presence at Portman Mansions and spent much of his time at his flat in Brighton, or travelling abroad. I also learned much later that when there was a crisis at the *Daily Express* forcing him to put in exceptionally long hours at the office, he booked a hotel near Fleet Street for convenience. His hotel of choice was The Savoy.

According to a *Daily Express* gossip column, which described him as a prime exponent of 'the razzamatazz school of journalism', he was planning to buy a plot of land on which to build a house on the Greek island of Skiathos, together with one of the *Express's* star writers whom he had originally discovered, the TV celebrity Nancy Spain. But although Susan Keeble travelled several times to Skiathos with Nancy Spain to explore the island and purchase land, in the end the Keebles divorced, Nancy Spain was killed in a plane crash in 1964 and the Skiathos dream withered and died.

During this extended period of turmoil, ill health and hospital admissions accounted for some of his absences. Once, Queenie mentioned in passing that he suffered from "heart problems" and was recuperating from a coronary thrombosis in 1963. Another time, she told me he was in the London Clinic for many weeks following a bout of severe pneumonia.

At the time, I too was on the move and, having left school, was increasingly away from home for extended periods. By the age of seventeen, I had embarked on a career in musical theatre and spent much of each year out of town and abroad, working in stage shows, TV, the occasional film and training in jazz dance in New York. In 1968, I was cast in a lead dance role in the West End production of the Broadway musical, *Promises, Promises*, and remained in the show throughout its two-year run.

The show had just opened when I bumped into Harold on the landing and to my surprise, since he had never previously shown any interest in my work, he asked whether I was working at that moment. When I told him about *Promises, Promises* at the Prince of Wales Theatre, he sounded interested, saying how much he enjoyed the Billy Wilder film *The Apartment*, on which the musical was based.

To my even greater surprise, a hand-delivered letter arrived one morning, shortly after our chat. He had evidently been to see *Promises, Promises* the previous evening.

Dear Alix,

You really are – and let's spell it out slowly and boldly underline it – ***quite terrific****! The vitality with which you dominate that First Act finalé is a joy to behold.*

I noticed my old sparring partner of earlier Daily Express days, m'Lord Snowdon, on the other side of the theatre. Did he pay you all a visit? I still see him quite often (in places as far apart as Tokyo and New York, not to mention here at home); I'll call him in the morning and see if he shares my enthusiasm about the show.

And I say it again – sincere congratulations!

Yours,
Harold

Considering we were on little more than nodding terms, I was delighted by his letter. Perhaps he only just realised I had grown up. I was therefore even more taken aback when another letter arrived several months later. Included was an article about the unusually prolific and popular American playwright Neil Simon.

Dear Alix,

Queenie, it must be officially recorded, shares my boundless enthusiasm for "Promises etc".

The Neil Simon success story is quite beyond belief: I thought you might be interested in the enclosed in today's "Time". I met him not long ago with Rosemary Harris when she was doing "Plaza Suite" – she's someone I've known for years.

I see you popping up on the box recently, with Cliff Richard – yes?

Please don't trouble to acknowledge this note and I don't need the "Time" clipping returned.

Best wishes as we surge into the Soaring Seventies (or whatever).

Yours,
Harold

When Queenie told me Harold had been ill again, and was forced to take time off work to rest, I sent him a get-well card. This time a reply came from Brighton.

Dear Alexandra,

Thank you so much for your "get well soon" note: I was most touched. I have been down here at my flat in Brighton, which I'm very fond of, hoping to convalesce fully.

Alas, alas, this heart of mine is playing me up and – imagine! – I have to be readmitted tomorrow, this time to the London Clinic where I was about ten weeks ago. I'm pretty fed up I can tell you.

But you – and your "great and good friend" as "Time" always puts it – we will make that 15-year-delayed dinner one of these days. [A jokey reference to a remark he once made in our hallway that my boyfriend and I should join him sometime for dinner, though obviously not as far back as fifteen years.]

Thanks again – and all good regards.

Yours,
Harold

* * *

Almost a year into Harold's optimistically dubbed 'Soaring Seventies', the run of *Promises, Promises* ended in late 1970. For the first time after the run of a show or TV series, a sense of anticlimax descended on my work life. It arrived out of the blue and mystified me, since otherwise everything else in my life was positive and upbeat. For almost a decade, my social activities and relationships revolved around show business and I revelled in the fast pace and unpredictability of theatre life, made crazier by the buzz of 1960s London.

I was also in my first serious relationship with a kind, loving, much older man, a divorcee, whose dearest wish was for us to live together or, better still, marry and settle down. But the term 'settling down', getting married, let alone having children was anathema to me and did not, at that stage, fit in with my vision of the future. I knew myself well enough to recognise our marriage would be doomed from the outset because of my immaturity and inexperience – and a genuine conviction that I needed to live and learn a lot more before I was ready to settle down. For now, being single and independent suited me perfectly and I loved it.

In my career, however, I knew I was approaching a crossroads. Always fiercely ambitious, I had worked, trained and performed solidly throughout the second half of my teens and early twenties, but I knew my choices as a performer were limited. A dancer's life is short and opportunities are few, especially in the UK, unlike America where dancers are given featured roles and can become stars of musical theatre.

There were other factors I had previously ignored, which took some gloss off the dance world. Unless they are members of an established classical or contemporary dance company, dancers are sometimes regarded as a lesser species compared to actors, musicians and singers. Of all artists, they are usually the worst paid, least respected, hardest working, most injury-prone and minimally protected by Equity union rules. Dancers also have the least voice – literally – in theatre and show business, and are expected to obey choreographers' orders unquestioningly, rarely contributing to the creative process.

For the first time, I saw how little control I had over my working life. I also realised I had too much untapped mental energy to continue in the essentially passive role of a freelance dancer 'for hire', waiting for the phone to ring and be summoned to an audition. I needed greater stimulus and bigger challenges, especially mental and intellectual ones. Prompted by gut instinct, I changed my agent and made a conscious decision to concentrate on getting acting work.

While I didn't recognise it at the time, it was a crucial turning point. Despite a dispiriting year of being largely out of work, followed by a slow start to acting in TV plays, embarking on this new route had a galvanising effect on my creativity: a jammed lock had snapped open to reveal the contents of a forgotten suitcase. Up bubbled unexpected interests, fresh ideas and flights of imagination clamouring for release. I had a brain, independent thought – and a voice. Surely there might be a way for me to use more of all three?

One thing led to another. Having begun acting, I also started writing, purely for pleasure and self-expression. From early childhood, I was always a bookworm, with an enormous appetite for any written material that came my way. My parents owned a large collection of books and they also bought almost every national and London newspaper. My Russian father, a painter, theatrical designer as well as a ballet impresario running his own companies, insisted on reading all the arts columns and latest theatre reviews, whether of his own productions or anyone else's. He therefore bought not only daily quality broadsheets like the *Times* but, on Sundays, also the mass market 'red tops'.

Added to this daily tsunami of newsprint that swept through our flat, my parents would stop by our local newspaper seller outside the Classic Cinema on the King's Road to buy all three London evening papers, *The Star*, *Evening Standard* and *Evening News*, with breaking news of that day's pea-souper fog, the latest grisly murders, royal scandals, industrial strikes and the deaths of kings and dictators. We also read *The Tatler*, *Illustrated London News* and *Picture Post,* which I loved as much for its quirky reports on British life as for its immersive photo reportage. As an only child with so much compelling material to feed the imagination, soon after I could read, I was on the way to becoming a five-year-old news junkie.

Now, when out of work, between rehearsals and breaks

in filming, I began writing on topics that especially interested me such as dance, fashion, women's health and lifestyles. Since my teens, I had read women's magazines from the American youth-focused *Seventeen* to *Nova* and *Vogue*, but also, since I spoke both languages, the most popular French and German glossies.

Every few weeks, I visited international newsagents in Soho to stock up on the latest foreign language publications – which sometimes included my grandmother's favourite Austrian gossip magazines. What struck me was the depth and breadth with which European journalists covered so-called 'women's issues', compared to the English press. In France especially, articles on women's appearance were always linked to health, lifestyle and medical conditions. I was introduced to the concept of physical appearance and inner health being inextricably linked, a philosophy summed up in the French expression, *se sentir bien dans sa peau* – to feel comfortable in one's skin. Nutrition, sex, reproductive health and emotional wellbeing featured regularly in *Marie Claire* and *Elle,* and by the Seventies, continental Europe seemed to have embraced the philosophy of 'holistic' health long before the movement took off in America.

Eventually, I began translating and rewriting the most original and interesting articles, imagining myself writing for a popular upmarket British magazine. It dawned on me that writing could become a 'second string' to my bow. Acting and writing seemed a good double-act. Given my background, I already had ambitions to be a dance critic and every time I went to the ballet or a contemporary dance show I got into the habit of writing a review of about eight hundred words, the average length of a newspaper review.

Lack of typing skills, pathetically using one finger to laboriously clack away on my mother's manual Olivetti, failed to dampen my enthusiasm. On the contrary, the novel experience of sitting at the kitchen table for hours poring over dictionaries, a thesaurus and other reference books instead of taking dance and singing classes or meeting friends, was vastly stimulating. As ideas germinated and took shape in my head, sprawled across my notepad, then rolled off the typewriter on crisp sheets of A4, I started to feel excited, especially at the sense of being in control. Telling a story in my own words was a heady challenge and I loved it.

Of course, I had no clue how to proceed from there, or indeed whether it was wise to proceed at all. How I might go about getting published was a mystery. Since I assumed that to have one's work published one had to take a course in journalism, have a university degree or begin as a junior reporter on a local newspaper – or perhaps all three – I saw no way into professional journalism. My academic qualifications were nil.

* * *

The thought of asking Harold Keeble for advice did not immediately occur to me and, when it drifted into consciousness, the idea seemed presumptuous, even ludicrous, given my inexperience. By now, I knew quite a bit more about Harold, and recognised that he was a highly respected Mr Big on Fleet Street. He had 'crossed the street' a number of times, like many editors and journalists who come and go and return again from one newspaper to another during the course of their career. Since the mid 1930s, he worked on and off for the *Daily Express* and *Sunday Express,* in every capacity from features editor, associate editor, editor and production executive; he jumped ship to the *Daily Mirror;* had a spell on the *Daily Sketch;* then moved back again to the *Daily Express* and was now ensconced at the *Daily Mail* as a 'special consultant'.

There, he became chief *consigliere* to David English, the young, pioneering editor who was on a mission to revamp the *Daily Mail* and turn it into the country's top selling popular newspaper – a position long held by the *Daily Express.*

In May 1971, the 150-year-old *Daily Mail* shed its fusty middle-England image and reinvented itself as a half-size 'compact' format – the term 'tabloid' was dismissed as vulgarly downmarket by the publishers – in a bid to attract a young, aspiring, cosmopolitan readership, with particular appeal to women. Harold, whose reputation as Fleet Street's finest design, layout and style expert remained second to none, was credited with helping David English create the eye-catching design and youthful irreverence of the new look *Daily Mail.* With the launch of its nudge-nudge wink-wink advertising campaign, *Every Woman Needs Her Daily Mail. And Every Man Knows Why*, the paper's female readership soon doubled and kept climbing.

With Harold in his pivotal role of chief editorial consultant at the *Daily Mail,* his flat again became a focus of activity, as in my school days. Comings and goings resumed at all hours of the day and night; as did deliveries of proofs, dummy layouts and newspapers.

Parked outside our block in Chiltern Street, Harold's previous saloon cars were replaced by a black, convertible Alfa Romeo which he happily drove around town with the hood down at all times of year – except when it rained. He only occasionally used a driver, and his present chauffeur seemed to be part-time driver, butler and general factotum.

One day, I was taken aback by a spontaneous invitation to bring my boyfriend, HR, to join him for drinks at his flat the following evening. I always wondered what his home was like in comparison to ours and found it was the exact mirror image of mine – only bigger and grander. Four sets of French windows in his double reception room opened onto long balconies, one facing the lights of Marylebone Road, the Planetarium and Madame Tussaud's, the other overlooking the bustling junction with Baker Street. After dark, both vistas were transformed into a glittering, Manhattan-style panorama.

The interior was understated ivory chic: deep pile carpets, cream velvet furnishings, wall-to-wall bookshelves and warm lighting. Ironically, it seemed to bear the signature of Mary Keeble's coolly elegant refinement. In fact, it was created by an interior design company hired by Scatty Susan, his second wife, who lacked both the design sense and organisational skills to mastermind the classy, pulled-together look.

Except for one striking anomaly. At the centre of this silken ivory sea, Harold had constructed for himself a sleek, sharp-edged modernist lair. Spotlit by a seven-foot, cantilevered chrome arc floor lamp designed by the Italian modernist Archille Castiglioni, stood a classic, black leather and chrome, Eames stretch-recliner with matching footstool. Scattered on the stool and surrounding carpet, in almost comic disarray, sheaves of photographs, contact sheets and transparencies jostled for space alongside books, record albums, newspapers and magazines.

Given the serene harmony of the rest of the room, this brazenly male zone had a life of its own and his housekeeper, Queenie, must have known better than to try and impose order on it. Harold's love of the minimalism of *Le Courbusier* and *Bauhaus* was all of a piece with his passion for cutting-edge technology. An exceptionally large television faced the stretch lounger and nearby, on a tripod, was a device I had only seen in TV and photographic studios but never in anyone's home. A self-confessed collector of the newest electronic gadgetry, he was evidently proud of his latest piece of kit, a video camera which could be connected, via another new acquisition, a video player, to his TV screen for instant playback.

Grinning mischievously, he explained, perhaps to see if he could shock us.

"It's the latest home movie technology. You film yourself, then play the footage back on the screen. And *voilà*, you see yourself in action!"

Cue laughter. We knew perfectly well what he meant. But, risqué as it sounded, Harold's evident glee over his new electronic toy removed any suggestion of smut from what was obviously intended as an instrument of seduction and voyeurism. Then again, given his obvious sense of devilry, maybe he was making it all up just to entertain us.

What struck me forcefully at that first proper social meeting was his directness; a wry humour spliced with blinding candour. As he gestured for us to sit down, and offered drinks from a generously stocked drinks trolley, I asked what he was having.

"My usual, tonic water," he laughed. "I'm sure you both would like something stronger."

"You're a teetotaller?"

"Far from it. Although I haven't drunk alcohol for many years. I can't. I'm an alcoholic."

He must have noted my surprise, more at his frankness than the disclosure. By that stage, I had known numbers of heavy drinkers and alcoholics including friends, two relatives and show business colleagues, even my own agent. True to form, all, without exception, strenuously denied having an alcohol 'problem'.

Bluntly, he admitted being diagnosed with a chronic cardiac disorder in the 1960s, and felt lucky at surviving a coronary thrombosis. The condition, one-sided atrial fibrillation, causes a potentially fatal irregular heartbeat which is brought on, as well as severely aggravated, by even moderate amounts of alcohol and greatly increases the risk of a heart attack or stroke.

"My doctor gave me an ultimatum. Continue drinking and you'll be dead within a year. Or stop now – today – is how he put it. It is the hardest challenge I have faced in my life, since the death of my first wife. And except for falling briefly off the wagon a few years ago, I haven't touched a drink. I won't even eat food, like trifle, if it's flavoured with alcohol."

It was the first proper social meeting I'd had with my neighbour, yet I felt as if I had known him for years. Perhaps my reticence about asking him for career advice was misplaced. He surely was the person to ask how I could go about getting some of my writing published – or even breaking into journalism. He was also best qualified to tell me to forget about writing and stick to show business.

2

Don't Worry If It's No Bloody Good

My letter to Harold was written in early October 1971.

Dear Harold,

I hope you don't mind me writing to ask your professional advice. For the last few months I have spent a lot of time, between auditions and rehearsals and being out of work, writing on a range of subjects which interest me in the theatre, women's lives, and fashion and beauty.

I find writing interesting, enjoyable and challenging and would love to write professionally if at all possible, hopefully combining it with acting work. Ideally, I would like to be a dance critic although I realise it is probably hard to break into that small, specialised field which seems to be monopolised by middle-aged or elderly men who have held their jobs for many years and remain enraptured by the twee, airy-fairy aesthetic of classical ballet. They seem to lack appreciation of new avant-garde trends in dance. I have therefore been writing reviews of dance companies I recently went to see.

Secondly, because I speak French and German, I cannot understand why there are so many subjects covered in foreign magazines which hardly get a mention in the British press. This led me to tackle several of these neglected subjects which I suspect have a wider and more commercial appeal than dance reviews.

I would be grateful if you could look at the enclosed pieces and let me know if you think I have any talent or a chance of eventually getting some articles published. Please don't worry if it isn't any bloody good. I won't be upset. After all, as you know, I already have a career in show business and writing is something that would probably only become, at best, a second string to my bow. Most importantly it would allow me to use my brain more than I do now.

Best wishes,

Alix

I enclosed half a dozen 'specimens', to give him some idea of the diversity of subjects I wanted to write about. They included a review of the Royal Ballet's new three act ballet, *Anastasia*, created by the company's Artistic Director, Kenneth MacMillan, starring Lynn Seymour, the world's greatest actress-ballerina

Another review was of *Flowers*, an outrageously camp dance and mime work by Lindsay Kemp and his company. Based on Jean Genet's homoerotic novel, *Our Lady of the Flowers*, it was a part grotesque, part surreal melodrama featuring transvestite characters in clown makeup, diaphanous gowns and scream-in-the-night hairstyles. The show had outraged and delighted audiences in equal measure and had critics clutching their pearls.

To give a flavour of other, frothier, subjects, I included a long article about cellulite, which I had only ever seen covered by

French magazines and several pieces on current fashion trends and how to adapt them.

I bundled the lot into an envelope with my letter and slid it beneath Harold's front door. It was the first time I had ever chosen to be judged, rather than being forced to face approval or rejection at an audition – and I liked the sense of agency that came with this new, elective type of interview. Then, thinking no further about it, I went off to begin rehearsals for a TV play in which I had just landed my first straight role.

I was taken aback by Harold's speedy response – there were two replies in rapid succession. Even more astonishing was his positive tone, even though I was alarmed to find he had returned all my articles.

Alix, dear Alix,

I have a phenomenal capacity for ballsing things up - agreed, agreed! But <u>bad manners</u> is a sin I try to dodge.

The truth: I live marooned under magazines and newspapers and your letter <u>got covered up</u>. Amen - with bowed head.

Alix, I'm not much of a judge (obviously, I'd say!) on this ballet writing area (the other items <u>do</u> interest me very much).

Please let me have the stuff back - if possible through the letter-box this evening - and I will take them to Brighton and, for what my opinion <u>is</u> worth, let you have it.

If I <u>can</u> help I'd like to.

Very sorry.

And for your patience - thanx.

Harold

A second letter, typed on *Daily Mail* stationery, arrived almost a week later.

Dear Alix,

Your flatmate told me you were out of London for a day or two – I hope enjoying yourself.

No, you are absolutely wrong in thinking the stuff is – in your own phrase – "no bloody good". Very much the reverse, I would say. I must emphasise again that the subject covers territory I don't understand, but quite clearly you have a feeling for words, a capacity to present coherent argument and a sense of structure.

The problem is: where is it to go? It's a persistent problem and never so daunting as it is now – for if the theatre is having its problems, then newspapers are, to the power of infinity!

I cannot honestly think of any paper interested in ballet which has not got staff coverage already. (Incidentally, I am absolutely certain you are right about people sounding off on this subject without any real knowledge to back them up.)

What I would like to do is to show the stuff to someone I know on the Observer – maybe you know the name, Kilmartin – whom I am seeing this weekend.

But on the other beauty idea, I think we might be able to do something with that on the "Mail". Why don't you pop in for a drink and we could go over it anyhow?

Best – and salutations to HR.

Harold

I had anticipated Harold's ambivalence about becoming a dance critic and saw it as realistic. He may not have known much about dance, but he knew about the privileged position of theatre critics and that the chances of a newcomer gatecrashing that elite were virtually nil.

When we next met, Harold agreed with me that dance criticism – like much arts coverage – needed a younger, fresher, irreverent eye.

"The problem is that they have all been there for a very, very long time, far too long, and they've reached the stage where they are all writing for each other, courting praise from the Critics Circle."

He'd got it in one.

Dear Alix,

Maybe we could meet sometime next week. It's nice of you to say I'm being helpful - but not really, until we can get something done, something into ink on paper.

Would you like to try your milk teeth on something for that little magazine I run? No staggering financial rewards but it would be ACTION!

See you around. And success with the audition! "Forum", presumably.

Harold.

When we next met, he showed me his 'little magazine', a glossy, high quality publication called *Chandelier* which he edited. It was produced by Trusthouse Forte for distribution in all their top hotels. Despite Harold's commitments at the *Daily Mail,* he had agreed to edit *Chandelier* partly as a favour to his friend and colleague David Wynne-Morgan, a leading advertising and public relations maven who at the time worked with Trusthouse Forte.

He came straight to the point. "How about writing a fashion feature for the next issue? Spring 1972. Would you be interested?"

While my grasp of the fashion industry was minimal, I didn't think twice about accepting. I reasoned that I could probably pick up new ideas and fashion trends by looking at trade press coverage of the recent Paris and New York collections, as well as the *Prêt-à-Porter* shows of younger, zingier designs likely to be reproduced cheaply on the high streets.

"Of course I'm interested."

He must have read my mind about not being an authority on the fashion business, and explained what he really wanted for the magazine was a bold, personalised approach; a fresh eye picking out upcoming trends for next spring and summer's 'look'. Ever the master of the splashy headline and provocative lead-in, he suggested a title for the piece: *I Predict,* in extra large, heavy type, to be followed by a series of statements about what I foresaw would be 'in' and on-trend in clothing, as well as accessories including jewellery, hats and shoes.

Harold urged me to start researching the spread immediately. There was no time to waste, as I had been engaged to choreograph a Dutch production of the Broadway musical, *A Funny Thing Happened on the Way to the Forum*, which was shortly going into rehearsal in Amsterdam, and would take up a fortnight of my time. So, in under three weeks, I had to find sales samples of fashions due to hit the stores by Spring 1972, choose a suitable selection and 'book' them for a photo session.

I was ignorant of the elements necessary to assemble a fashion feature, but he assured me he would schedule the photo shoot and choose a photographer for the job. The photographer would book the model. However, it was up to me to find the clothes and accessories, arrange to 'reserve' a selection of these for the photo session, and return them afterwards to the retailer, public relations company, or fashion company who had lent them to us.

At that point, I knew I was jumping into the deep end. Which retailers? Who were the fashion buyers at the big department stores? Did one have to first approach fashion PR companies? And wouldn't the manufacturers, big names like Jaeger and Mary Quant, refuse to lend their precious samples to a complete novice who had never written a line of journalism, let alone a fashion feature?

Fortunately, an old friend came to the rescue. Stewart Grimshaw, a stunningly handsome and elegant young Scotsman, the long-time partner of Simon Sainsbury from the eponymous grocery empire, and who owned Provans, a fashionable restaurant in Chelsea, suggested I call his friend Ann Boyd, whom I had met socially. A graduate of St Martin's College of Art, Ann was a fun, straight-talking Scotswoman and the senior fashion buyer at Miss Selfridge. Stewart assured me she would have sample stock and was likely to help me borrow what I needed for the *Chandelier* fashion shoot.

He was right. Ann was a fashion pro with all the necessary inside information I lacked, and it helped that we already knew one another. While happy to put me on the right road, she didn't pull any punches. "If you are going to do this spread, I am sure you want to do it properly, otherwise it isn't worth doing," she said bluntly, persuading me it would be simpler all round if I borrowed all the clothes to be photographed from Miss Selfridge, once I had chosen items from her stockroom samples for the following season.

Apart from the Miss Selfridge line, all the shop's other fashions came from different manufacturers. Not only would selecting everything from under one roof make the borrowing and eventual return of the clothes a lot easier, but she could help me achieve a cohesive, pulled-together look. New jewellery, shoes and hats on order for the following year were finally added to the clothes.

The photographer, Chris Barham, whom Harold picked from the *Daily Mail's* pool of photographers to do the *Chandelier* spread, booked two models and asked me to arrive at the studio well ahead of the shoot to pick out combinations of clothes and accessories I wanted him to photograph. This part of the process, working on the look and theme of the piece, felt very familiar and reminded me of costume fittings and dress rehearsals which are an integral part of mounting a stage or TV show. Once the models arrived, tried on the clothes and Chris started shooting, improvising several variations of a 'look', the atmosphere and focus on technical details of lighting, costume detail and styling was no different from theatre and TV work.

The pictures looked good. My article took shape once I had enough inside information to 'predict' fashion trends for the following year. When Harold got my copy, he seemed pleased and had only a few criticisms and corrections.

Dear Alix,

No question about it: with a bit of luck (and no union troubles!) you'd soon make a go in this field. With a good editor (because there are some touches of technique to learn) you'd soon be up, up and away.

Most pleased with this: it's what I wanted, anyway.

Points:

X The intro I could trim a bit and I think out with the oft said "Anything goes..." phrase and any other which seems stale.

X Would welcome a few more purely personal things, eg. the collar-bone quote, etc.

X Phrase "Cleavage exposed" must be wrong, tautologous or whatever! Cleavage is the art of exposing, not something you expose, like... well, no matter: not serious.

X More serious is just getting the thing finished and pictures selected, meaning just getting together, as I've got myself lumbered with two dinners I could well do without and you've got your problems and there's a bloody war in India and so on. Week's end (as "Time" says) is OK but I'll continue to telephone you until we connect up.

But going fine, Alix: and I'll do my best to get you beyond modest "Chandelier".

H

Here, for Robin [Robin Lang, a flatmate of mine with strong Marxist leanings] *is the "Daily Jang", new for the war, and may well be his scene. The "Daily JANG", it's an irresistible title somehow.*

Harold

PS. Oh yes, when you come to type it coulds't please manage double spacing and break up these formidably long paragraphs a bit? Thanx.

* * *

By the time I got back from a fortnight's rehearsals for *A Funny Thing Happened on the Way to the Forum* in Amsterdam, Harold alerted me to some production hiccups on the Spring issue of *Chandelier.*

Dear Alix,

I don't know what the hell came over Chris Barham. Even reduced, the lady sitting cross-legged still looks like one of those advertisements: ***Evening Classes. Principal. Strict Disciplinarian.*** *We shall have to do something.*

'I PREDICT' should be 'I predict' in lower case letters, they've forgotten the sub-deck of the heading and spelt your name wrongly! Yak!

I have the whole 36 pages to paste up – delivered at unexpected speed.

Telephone me when you surface, will you? Let's have lunch if you wish (lateish?); but understand if you can't. Hell, tho', if it's going to be weather like this, I wish you were in Brighton.

H

Later, he invited me to watch him pasting up my feature. Obviously, the whole technical and visual aspect of producing a publication excited him – and the excitement was contagious. I too became fired up with the fun of watching him lay out the two-page spread, experimenting with different sized fonts and typefaces, scribbled here and there to assemble a rough design. He worked fast, trying out different ideas – as I had seen my father experiment with hasty doodles and preparatory sketches that eventually morphed into a full-scale theatrical set.

In a similar way, Harold continued ripping out, scrunching up and throwing aside sheet after sheet of paper until he was happy with the layout. As he picked the photos and placed them amid the text, then chopped up my copy into ten short, punchy paragraphs each headed *I predict*, it was self-evident why he had acquired fame as Fleet Street's 'master' of layout and design.

He was also a total perfectionist, something I eventually realised was rare in an editor, especially in their dealings with individual journalists.

Dear Alix,

I've now been carefully thro' the fashion piece. It's very well done, Alix, really packing in a lot of information. You'd soon be off the ground (to repeat myself!) in this field . Nevertheless - because I want it to be a piece you might use for 'exhibition' purposes - I have three or four points (mainly excisions) I'd like to go over with you if I may: perhaps later this morning - I'm in ALL morning and I'll ring you about 11 o'clock.

I also have an idea for you for the next edition

Salutations. Harold

PS. Brace yourself! Can you face another? Again, I fear, only £25 but it can - indeed <u>must</u> - all be done in a day; it is in fact virtually a re-write job based on a brochure but calling for either one visit to the Tower Bridge area or maybe just some telephone calls. Deadline tomorrow evening.

Aware he had a fledgling hack living next door, he seemed to relish the role of mentor and started to pass the odd eleventh hour 'rush job' my way. Might I like to bang out a couple of hundred words for a modest fee? Just a brief 'cuttings job'? Re-jigging and 'journalising' some marketing or PR material? If, as in this specific case, I turned down his request, Harold entirely understood, aware that I knew my own limitations as a writer.

These limitations included working very fast under pressure to a tight deadline, especially when the subject was unfamiliar to me, as with the 'Tower Bridge' request. This was truly something of which I knew nothing – the launch of *HMS Belfast* as a 'Museum Ship', an offshoot of the Imperial War Museum, moored on the Thames by the Tower of London. The public opening of *HMS Belfast* was especially newsworthy for the foreign tourists and visitors who read *Chandelier*: it was London's newest tourist attraction and had recently been saved from demolition after a major campaign to save it as a historic British monument. Fortunately, my flatmate Robin Lang, a graduate of LSE, who knew Harold as a neighbour, did the last minute rewrite and produced an authoritative, well-written piece within the allotted twenty-four hours.

By the end of the production process, I felt I had taken a beginner's crash course in journalism and magazine publishing from an expert tutor. What I did not expect at the end of it all was the final reward. When Harold showed me the dummy issue – a preview of the finished magazine – I felt a thrill familiar to every journalist and author when they first see their work in print beneath their name, or byline as it is known in the trade.

Three months later, when *Chandelier* was distributed to the Trusthouse Forte hotels, Harold left a copy outside my door with a message scribbled in green above my name on the fashion spread.

> *It is quite gratifying how <u>well</u> this stood up. Don't give up too easily. Love H*

3

The Editor's New Clothes

THE FIRST TIME Harold invited me out to dinner, I thought he wanted to discuss ideas for future articles. But early in the meal, *a propos* of nothing in particular, he mentioned he was recently on his balcony and spotted me with HR down in Chiltern Street setting off for the theatre. Typically, he hadn't missed a trick.

"It's impossible not to notice how HR's look has changed over the past years. He seems to have an entirely new wardrobe. Very stylish. More colourful. Would this be your influence?"

I was flattered by his observation. Much as I enjoyed shopping for clothes by myself, discovering and trying on new fashions, it was as much fun, albeit more challenging, to go on shopping expeditions with a boyfriend – especially one like HR, who was as enthusiastic as I was about revamping his own wardrobe.

Harold pursued the Pygmalion theme further. "You have great taste in fabrics and colour co-ordination. Did you choose all those pink, purple and striped shirts and the contrasting ties?"

I nodded.

"My goodness, you've transformed him. He's gone from a sober-suited businessman to a stylish gent about town. It's nothing less than the transmogrification of HR."

There was a long pause.

"I don't suppose you could do something similar for me...?"

It was the last question I expected. Revamp the wardrobe of a much older man, old enough to be my father, not my husband or boyfriend? Could it be done? More to the point, could I pull it off?

He admitted he paid scant attention to his clothes, or to men's fashion generally. He chose styles, fabrics and colours that were classic, safe, of high quality – and slightly dull. Black trousers, white shirt, dark tie, a black or navy V-necked cardigan: very Professor Higgins. Outdoors, he wore a black mackintosh which, as I teasingly remarked, reminded me of that worn by the controversial prison reformer Lord Longford, who had recently been photographed by the press, and this became a running gag between Harold and me. These were the staples of his modest work outfit, suitable for getting 'down and dirty' at the office.

There was a logic to it. As a specialist in layout and design, his work could be physical, even messy, more the toil of an artist than a wordsmith. He would create layouts standing at a lectern, on a large board covered with foolscap or tracing paper. Using different coloured crayons to highlight the desired effects, he experimented with the placing of banner headlines and introductory 'blurbs' and which size and style of font worked best, sketching in the photos with their captions, and dividing up columns of print. Working fast, with bold, sweeping strokes, he would tear up pages and begin all over again if the effect didn't please him.

The largely black outfit didn't show the dirt and charcoal or crayon marks, and he usually rolled up his shirt sleeves for greater freedom of movement, which is why he never wore cufflinks at work. Sometimes, he put on a leather driving glove to better grip the crayons, but any other accessories that might impede his wrist and hand movements were a non-starter.

I agreed to organise a fashion makeover, took out my diary

and asked if he wanted to make a date for us to go shopping. He didn't; he already had a plan. There would be no trawling around London visiting every possible men's fashion store. His choice of venues was narrow and exclusive: Jermyn Street and Piccadilly. The shops were equally up-market: Turnbull and Asser, Simpsons and possibly Hawes and Curtis. Harrods was another possible destination.

Because he had accounts at all four stores, my job was to peruse the contents of each of them and look for shirts, ties, and perhaps pullovers, cardigans and scarves, with a view of putting together a modern 'look'. I was to pick a selection of garments and the cost would be added to his accounts on a 'payment on approval' basis and I would bring them back home to Baker Street, where he could choose which, if any, he liked.

He suggested it might be a good idea for me to bring extra fabric samples to widen the choice. The sole exception to this plan was that we might arrange a Saturday visit to Harrods together so I could help him choose a new suit or two.

Realising I was free to pick and choose according to my own taste, I couldn't wait to embark on the mission. Not that his new wardrobe was meant to replace his monochrome work outfits; it was to provide a more stylish alternative for social and casual occasions, of which I guessed there were more than he let on.

Once I hit Jermyn Street, I tried to visualise the kinds of non-work occasions and social circles for which he might want to wear more striking outfits. The clothes had to be stylish, modern, yet quietly elegant, nothing too garishly flamboyant or outré by way of design. But what actually *was* his social life? Clearly, I wasn't updating the image of someone undergoing a mid-life crisis, a man in late middle age foolishly dreaming of cutting a trendy figure in night clubs, discos or the fleshpots of the Riviera.

But I had little idea as to how, where and with whom he did relax. An intensely private man, he lived his life in a series of hermetically sealed compartments, making it difficult to distinguish between the realms of work, relaxation, domesticity and personal relationships. There was no doubt that he was a workaholic, a creature of the night who might also, however, be up at dawn since he went into the *Daily Mail* at the oddest hours of day or night. Yet from his letters I deduced that he fitted in regular social engagements, trips out of town and foreign travel.

As for his love life, that too remained a mystery, since he never mentioned the existence of anyone special on the scene. Although from time to time attractive women appeared to come and go, none occupied the role of live-in partner or mistress.

Dearest Alix,

Thanx your note. I hope you had a good evening.

As a reminder, here is the shirt to be copied, without the floral decoration. ***One*** *of those.*

The others were:

2 of the houndstooth job

2 more of the stripe on stripe of the chiffon job.

And that's it!

Except for these short, dragging sleeves...

And of course the major leap forward into the cufflink set. I've been noticing the point you made. [I thought the right cufflinks instantly updated a sober-looking shirt.]

You are right. You usually are.

Can I see these interview pieces, please?

Love

Harold

I seemed to have passed the test, steering the right balance between trendy and traditional. He gave me the green light to continue the mission.

Darling Alix,

I notice that blue blind drawn at 10.30: this is what makes me sick with envy and you radiantly good-looking.

Listen. My thanx for doing the T&A [Turnbull & Asser] *chore for me. Keep an eye open for a silk (mock silk?) dressing gown for under £103. Reason for asking you – well, as you see, my judgement is poor; but also I wanted to test what I've always suspected to be very strong. ie. your self-assurance. It is a responsibility to commit me to that much money, sight unseen. And what I bloody well admire is your willingness and readiness to do it!!! I mean this and I'm grateful and what you say goes and I'll be totally honest and utterly uncomplaining about the result. Surprise me ! No snips of patterns – just the finished stuff. (Only one request: not too dark colours, yes?)*

I find this rather fun.

I'll ring you sometime late afternoon.

Here is the letter to Reynolds which please read.

Harold

* * *

AS I GOT to know him better, I had the impression Harold's social life was not only livelier than he let on, but also that it made more inroads into his work schedule than he wanted. It was obvious he hated an over-hectic lifestyle, often grumbling that he did too much in a day or the course of the week, getting to bed too late, entertaining too often and working excessively long hours, especially when he wasn't feeling his best.

He knew his main fault was being a man who 'can't say no' – crucially, he recognised this was dangerous to his health, a warning continually hammered home by his doctor whom he described as a "strict disciplinarian". I felt bad about occasionally adding to his task-load by pitching ideas for articles – which required more of his attention since they were for *Chandelier* and, on a long-shot basis, potentially for the *Daily Mail.*

Darling Alix,

What you ask isn't so bloody easy. To my fury, this particular issue of "Elle" has vanished from the "Mail" (where they should have three copies) and from my flat.

The 'head bandage' idea could have good headline possibilities but I'm not quite clear on what it would embrace; and we ought to fix it before (and if) I go away. Isn't it a bit late in the year for the sunglasses bit? I'm not sure – what say you?

It was Bad Day at Black Rock for me yesterday & I was very late back. My glasses (apart from being wrongly addressed) have arrived – smashed to bits. I had to take someone to lunch at Odin's, someone to dinner at Boulestin's & I hate overeating... but who's to blame for that except me!

Furthermore, any thoughts (laughter!) of "a few quiet days in Leningrad" [he had mentioned a possible working trip to the Soviet Union] *now seem distant. They simply will not grant me a visa because of two articles in the "Daily Mail". I could – with just today left – possibly get a tourist visa by lying about whom I work for, but the idea of that coming to light, alone in Leningrad, doesn't appeal to me much.*

HOW ARE YOU SLEEPING? It's 10.20 and your blinds, I'm happy to see, are still drawn. Alix-in-Darkness

Appreciate Saturday shopping session. It's the real stuff, alas – non-shabby suits – I'm short of. Are you often very ashamed of being seen around with me? You so dead-target contemporary, me so otherwise.

Does Saturday rule out dinner tonight (I'm certainly facing no food before then!). At some time I have to go to Brighton, a swift there-&-back.

Alix, dear Alix, we'll be in touch.
Sleep fast - we need the pillows...
H

* * *

DETAILS SLOWLY EMERGED about his private life and who he shared it with, although the overall picture remained sketchy. What I learnt, however, was more colourful and unconventional than I previously supposed. He counted Molly and Peter Daubeny, the impresario, among his closest friends. Sir Peter Daubeny was a respected theatrical producer renowned for founding the annual World Theatre Season at the Aldwych Theatre. Each season featured a programme of classical and contemporary drama from around the world, staged by starry international directors and featuring major foreign actors performing in their native language. Headsets were distributed to audiences so they could hear a simultaneous English translation of the text.

Harold always tried to see several of these plays and, to my delight and surprise, it turned out that he was far more of an arts enthusiast and theatregoer than I realised. Another of his intimates was Lionel Green, founder of the Windsmoor womenswear brand, a hugely successful company regarded as the epitome of British women's tailoring, fabric and heritage. Lionel Green, a divorcee who subsequently remarried a much younger woman, lived 'above the shop', the company's Mayfair headquarters, and although Windsmoor concentrated chiefly on women's fashions, he was Harold's chief *consigliere* on men's fashion designers, retailers and prices.

Inevitably, Harold's social life was a blend of business and pleasure. He would relay snippets of conversations after having dinner with "the boss", the current Lord Rothermere – Vere Harmsworth – who owned the *Daily Mail.* They were on first-name terms and Vere was by all accounts a refreshingly unstuffy and open-minded newspaper proprietor who, unlike other press barons, left his editors to run the newspaper with minimal interference and maximum encouragement. Vere apparently also shared Harold's conviction that women must constitute the target readership of any successful modern newspaper

Unlike many editors and newspapermen of that time, Harold leant instinctively towards the offbeat and the creative rather than pillars of the establishment, or the grey uniformity of the business world. Some of his closest friendships developed from working relationships and dated back to his days on the *Daily Express* and his editorship of the *Sunday Express*. There, in the late 1940s and 1950s, he had worked closely, and socialised, with the paper's cartoonists Carl Giles and Osbert Lancaster, fashion illustrator Andrew Robb, show business columnist David Lewin and the columnist Nancy Spain.

Also in the 1950s, keen to follow America's lead by featuring more photo reportage in British newspapers, he launched an illustrated spread in the *Daily Express*, called *PhotoNews* and championed the work of many photographers, including a talented young freelancer, Tony Armstrong-Jones, who also went on to become a good friend. The two men remained close even after Armstrong-Jones's marriage to Princess Margaret – despite the fact that she reportedly ridiculed Harold's Yorkshire accent, which I, with my acute ear for accents, had failed even to notice. Far more distinctive was his husky, almost gravelly voice, projecting immediate energy and engagement.

Another of his 'finds' from the 1950s which turned into a friendship and transformed the *Express's* fashion pages, was the upcoming photographer John French, also a talented painter, who had developed an innovative way of using 'bounced' natural-looking light to highlight the model and the details of the clothes. When Harold commissioned a one-off photo from French for the *Express* fashion pages, the visual effect was so startlingly transformative that French's commissions immediately multiplied and his career took off.

When the two men became friends, Harold was invited to

lunch by French and his wife Vera Denning, a fashion journalist, to their weekend bolthole, a light and spacious seafront flat in Brighton. At the time, he could not guess that this very flat, with its large terrace overlooking the seafront, would eventually become his own second home.

That came about fortuitously through Harold's friendship with another fashion tycoon, the Irish couturier Digby Morton and his wife Phyllis, ten years Harold's senior. Phyllis Digby Morton, dubbed the '*Grande Dame of the Glossies*', was a trailblazing woman's editor before the war. In 1930, aged twenty-nine, she was appointed editor of a new magazine, *Home and Beauty* and became one of the best-known fashion and beauty journalists of her time, going on to write Britain's first 'agony aunt' column, covering every subject including sexual problems. After John French's death in 1966, his widow Vera moved out of their Brighton home and sold the remainder of the Brighton lease to Digby Morton and Phyllis, who promptly moved to the Cayman Islands and sold the remainder of their lease to Harold.

The women in Harold's life were harder to spot than the married couples and male friends. Although he loved female company, it was difficult to identify any unattached women who might be in the running for more than friendship. After the break-up of his second marriage to Sue, he mentioned the existence of one or two past girlfriends but without any suggestion of a long-term relationship

Among older women journalists of his own generation who drifted in and out of his orbit, some were married to newspapermen, like the American writer and editor of *Style* magazine, Fleur Cowles, wife of a publishing tycoon and editor of *Look*, one of Harold's favourite US photo reportage magazines.

Of a similar vintage was the American *doyenne* of agony aunts, Elizabeth Winship, married to the editor of the *Boston Globe* newspaper. Harold's primary friendship was with the eccentric Thomas Winship, known as 'Mike', a droll character famed for his flamboyant flowered bow ties and red braces, who shunned all offers of a company limousine and insisted on driving a battered pick-up truck everyday to the *Globe* offices. Elizabeth landed an advice column, *Ask Beth*, in her husband's newspaper in 1963 and found nationwide fame when the column was syndicated by seventy US newspapers, making her the country's most sought-after and candid expert on sexual and relationship matters.

While the Winships came to London once a year, during the time Harold put me in charge of his new wardrobe, Mike was booked on a UK lecture tour, leaving Elizabeth to see friends in London. That included Harold, whose memory of her penetrating voice obliterated her other qualities. Which is why he invited me to join him when she asked him to have lunch with her, but advised me to "bring your earplugs".

Dear Alix,

I'm sorry if I showed a trace of irritability about the table last night

When I finally got back I had a quiet 50 minutes with "Sail Away". [I had lent him my LP of the 1960s musical written by Noel Coward which, when I saw it in my teens, impressed me with its witty lyrics and a punchy performance by the American musical actress Elaine Stritch.] *In its pre-Beatle way, what talent and charm in the lyrics and what a low-power candle power effort Miss Stritch's is in "Company"* [the Stephen Sondheim musical that had just opened in the West End] *compared to this!*

And speaking of Miss Stritch, the Winships are now booked in at the Ritz for three days next week. Would I like to go to dinner? And would I like to bring my goddaughter? "No" to the first; "Yes" to the second. [Asked by Mrs Winship if he wanted to bring someone, he passed me off as his goddaughter to avoid speculation.]

On the Brighton front (no pun intended), I intend when I finally get there (about 1pm or so!) to adopt a brazenly brisk posture. "Well now, hadn't we better get to grips with this thing? Aren't we dragging our feet a bit?" [His landlord was delaying overdue refurbishment of the shabby interior communal parts and other repairs to the house where he rented the first floor flat.] *But I still haven't got the real red herrings assembled on the slab, the real blueprint for chaos.*

These bloody tickets are for Saturday.

But cocktails at Hamleys - ah, that's my style. And so are you.

Morning!

H

PS. Remain totally pleased with my peacock dressing gown in dawn's early light. Thanx. Do you remember the big black hat worn by the seducer of Diana Rigg's stand-in? Is that the kind of job you got HR into? [The hat in question, a broad-brimmed fedora, was worn by a character in Tom Stoppard's *Jumpers*.]

* * *

Harold's fashion makeover proceeded apace. I went to Jermyn Street several times on my own to choose shirts, ties and a dressing gown, and joined him on two outings to Harrods to look at suits – with a detour to a couple of nearby jewellers for some new cufflinks. As he became more adventurous, he decided it was time to swap his old quartz watch for something smarter for special occasions, and sent me off to Walton Street with two of his finest old mechanical watches to have them serviced and repaired.

His remark about the hat worn by a character in *Jumpers* – and whether this was the style I had encouraged my boyfriend HR to wear – suggested he was throwing caution to the winds and contemplating a replacement for his battered fedora, the same one he wore on the day I first met him as a schoolgirl. Like me, Harold loved hats, which even led him to consider buying me one I noticed in a bohemian-style boutique owned by Martha Hill when we were walking along Marylebone High Street.

Darling Alix,

So it seemed an amusing flick-of-the-wrist gesture to pop into that shop and buy you the old bowler with the tatty feather.

It was £50.

I didn't buy it, feeling nonetheless the sting of stinginess, considering your lavish expenditure at T&A on my behalf. (Lionel has fooled me about the price.)

"This part of the shop, m'dear," said Martha herself, "pulls in the actresses: you'd be amazed."

*I **was**, more or less.*

*It **may** be that I'll have to meet you there – at the Cavendish: I'll **try** not to, probably succeed.*

I have booked a table again at Odin's – it's that timid, unadventurous black-tie mentality again.

Bring your earplugs for Mrs Winship [the American journalist we were supposed to be lunching with].

H

Odin's, a quiet elegant restaurant in Marylebone, was one of Harold's favourite venues, along with more traditional establishments like The Savoy Grill, The Caprice, Prunier's and the White Tower and had the advantage of being less than five minutes' drive from Portman Mansions.

While Harold liked to cultivate an 'old fogey' image, going out of his way to avoid trendy haunts and refusing to join elite clubs, this did not mean he was uninterested in celebrities and celebrity gossip: it was, after all, the bread and butter of his trade. In fact he thrived on breaking news, rumour and intrigue. Once he discovered that I had several connections to certain theatrical 'stars', he made sure to pass on the latest gossip and share any news that piqued both our interests.

Your Highness,

Here is a letter to your mum. Without my office book I never can remember that farm address. Here's a stamped envelope if you could fill it in. [A thank-you letter to my mother for asking him down for Sunday lunch.]

Perhaps on Saturday, when you're in the Walton Street belt, you'd be kind enough to drop these two watches into Hooper Bolton, & even, en route back in the cab, pick up the World Theatre Season prog from 26 Chester Square.

A bit about bitchy Stritchy here for you.

Mrs Winship is the original American horror. It was like lunching on the launch pad at Cape Kennedy during lift-off. [I could not join him for that lunch because of work.]

Decided I'm doing too much!

Love, H

4

You Pronounce It 'Sell-You-Leet'

By the time my first journalistic effort rolled off the presses, Harold and I had met socially several times, either for dinner or the occasional drink at his place, usually to discuss ideas for articles that might work in the *Daily Mail.* He seemed genuinely eager to help me get a break and, as he put it, "Get you into ink on paper". Having already offered me another double page spread in the summer issue of *Chandelier*, which I began writing early in 1972, he was always up for discussing any ideas I came up with. Aware how very much I had to learn, I became a sponge, absorbing knowledge at the feet of the master.

Dear Alix,

I'm taking you seriously! If I can be of help I'd like to; but it's this 'breaking in' which isn't easy.

Now take that restaurant idea of yours. It could be built up quite well.

THE RESTAURANT BUG: Why does it bite so many interestingly different people? [I told him I was surprised how many non-restaurateurs were successfully starting fashionable restaurants; they included the film director John Schlesinger, literary agent David Conville, the artist Apicella and my Scottish friend Stewart Grimshaw, a former chemist at Unilever.]

To give you some guidelines (not actually the two girls I'd choose), I enclose a couple of cuttings which you might like to read and then ask yourself honestly if you could meet this standard – or could fairly soon.

I <u>haven't</u> chosen <u>outstanding</u> stuff but competent, soundly-structured jobs which are not as easy to come by as you'd think. (The restaurant idea could be a dreadful drag if it were loosely done without bite or direction.)

Take the straight-on interview with Rowse. All <u>quotes</u> – and there's (perhaps wisely) a move these days to cutting off the superfluous descriptive 'fat' on pieces like this and getting right down to what the guy has to say. <u>This</u> too is not as easy as it looks – that is if you're going to report him accurately and with balanced emphasis.

Take the Ann Leslie stuff. A fair specimen of reasonably polished technique, dealing with difficult people, difficult questions and in circumstances of considerable distraction; <u>very</u> considerable distraction.

Take a look at these when convenient (actually they're library cuttings – at least Ann Leslie – and mustn't be missing too long).

Ask yourself how you'd really structure the idea of "Where Did The Musical Vanish?" [Another idea I came up with.] *It's fairly easy to write 'think-piece' essays. Not many newspapers <u>want</u> 'think-piece' essays.*

As I said before, I have a notion you'd make swift headway in this world: more so since talking to you. Will you push these clips thro' my letter box when you can?

I'm a bit involved early in the week but will give you a call and we'll take it from there. The thing is to get into print. Repeat: if I can help - well, gladly! Harold

* * *

OUR 'PITCHING SESSIONS', and Harold's afterthoughts, sparked lively conversations as we bounced ideas around. For me, these informal meetings with a newspaperman of Harold's stature were an intellectual and creative turn-on. Now over sixty, he had the curiosity, enthusiasm and open mind of a far younger man. Not only was I flattered by his interest in putting flesh on the bare bones of my ideas, the self respect and confidence I also gained by being listened to and encouraged, though still only a novice, was a wholly new experience.

And then there were the letters and messages. Like his conversation, Harold's letters –even one-liners hastily scribbled on a torn sheet of foolscap – fizzed with energy and anticipation. They would land at all hours of day or night in my letterbox or lie outside the front door, often on top of a pile of the latest newspapers, magazines, books, even records which he thought would interest me. Invariably written in bold longhand with felt-tipped pens of various colours – red, green or brown were his favourites – sometimes on contrasting coloured paper, he was ever the master of presentation. The words leapt off the page.

Dear Alix,

I didn't get your note until late: it lay on the table here.

"Ambassador". [I had free seats for a new musical based on Henry James's *The Ambassadors* and invited him to join me.] *Yes please - I'd like to go any place with you. ("The Mousetrap" even.) Only thing: Wednesday & Friday difficult.*

I'm intrigued by this full page for Clinique in the E/S. [The Evening Standard.] *(The very name of the stuff, Clinique, reflects the point you were arguing so very interestingly.) The girl in the picture – no languid bird waiting to be pressed on the cool sheets by a cosmetic-intoxicated man. The whole tone of the voice of the copy. Clearly Miss Kirsta is a girl ahead of her time.*

Clearly, too, from the restaurant stuff (tho' precisely WHERE still pitches a question mark), you're rapidly going to master the technique of construction, lead-in, pace and so on. It reads very well.

About this and the cellulite piece [another idea I pitched him much earlier] *which I'm sure we can do something about – it does have something to say.*

I'll telephone you, well I'll telephone you anyway...

Harold

* * *

AROUND THAT TIME, someone gave me an old 1969 copy of *Campaign* magazine, the advertising industry bible. On the front page was a photo of Harold and a long article about why he had resigned from his post as Executive Director of Publicity for Beaverbrook Newspapers. Unlike his previous roles as a journalist and editor, that last elevated title had put him in charge of the *Sunday Express* and *Daily Express's* advertising and marketing division. For several years, he had successfully promoted and updated the newspapers' profile through cinema and TV commercials, boosting circulation. It was a powerful position and when he stepped down from it, he also gave up his seat on the executive board of Express Newspapers; effectively ending a twenty-five-year relationship with the Beaverbrook empire.

What caught my eye in the article, however, was the reason for his resignation. His mission had been apparently to pursue a 'youth angle' in creating cinema and TV commercials to promote a less middle-aged, fusty image of the newspapers, but he was stymied by the dead hand of senior management, the men in grey suits upstairs who preferred to play safe. When he was blocked from hiring a more irreverent go-ahead advertising agency of his choice, he realised it was time to go.

It made me realise how often Harold's ideas, and his responses to my ideas, sprung from a commercial 'advertiser's eye' and an awareness of the growing trend in product 'branding'. He was convinced that women, especially young working women with disposable incomes, were crucial in determining the freshness and broad appeal of a newspaper. Being receptive to women's opinions and their changing lifestyles marked him out as unusually progressive, in contrast to the macho ethos that lingered in Fleet Street's editorial offices at the time.

I think that's why we got on so well. Once he discovered that I held relatively unconventional views on fashion, beauty, relationships, feminism and other so-called 'women's issues', it led to some lively discussions, even on a topic as lightweight as skincare. I found traditional representations of beauty – mask-like, over elaborate makeup, heavily lacquered helmet hairstyles, fussily packaged scented cosmetics and overcomplicated, time-consuming beauty regimes – widely outdated and off-putting to women of my generation. Even the infantilised wide-eyed image of the 1960s 'dolly bird', baby-faced and vacuous, had outlived its shelf life and was cringingly passé.

It also seemed that England was way behind the times compared to other countries. A backlash against cosmetic artifice had already emerged in parts of Europe, principally France, with a focus on good health and fitness as the main route to achieving healthy skin, hair and body, and the beauty industry had begun to reflect that ethos. The French tradition of selling cosmetics and skincare products in pharmacies, and the fact that top-selling ranges like Vichy, La Roche-Posay, Biotherm and Evian, had their origins in 'Thelassotherapy' seawater clinics and thermal spas, meant that their products stood out because of their simple, clinical packaging.

By the Seventies, in beauty branding, less had become more. These no-nonsense, uncomplicated products could have come straight out of a laboratory and were far removed from the baroque, sculpted glass jars of heavily scented unguents normally seen in English beauty salons.

This quasi-medical aesthetic was also taking off in the United States. In the late 1960s, the privately owned Estée Lauder empire launched the country's first 100% non-allergenic skincare range in collaboration with a leading New York dermatologist, Dr Norman Orentreich. The name of the range said it all. Clinique consisted of just a few key products: a soap-style cleansing bar complete with face brush for a heavy duty wash; a clarifying liquid containing medical grade hydroxy acids to remove accumulated skin debris; a fast-absorbed moisturising lotion suitable for all skin, designed not to irritate skin or block the pores.

Clinique became a bestseller in the US, Europe and the UK, especially among younger women who wanted a rapid, zero-fuss skincare routine and preferred to show off a glowing, healthy complexion instead of covering it up. Achieving a 'natural look', as opposed to a painted mask, was the on-trend message for women as the new decade got under way.

While trying to find my feet on the nursery slopes of journalism, it didn't occur to me to focus on any particular niche subject, despite my interest in health and beauty. The ideas I put to Harold were infinitely varied. They included what makes men and women bad timekeepers, especially when a man habitually turns up late for a date; why so many women are put off by men who try too hard to impress them by being overly polite and eager to please – a type I dubbed the 'Creepy Gents Brigade' – and why Broadway musicals are slicker and more successful than British ones. Inevitably, some ideas took off while others fell by the wayside. But, however offbeat my suggestions, he always came back with a response.

Dear Alix,

Thanx, darling, for your kind note of reassurance about the Creepy Gents Brigade. Alas, facts are stubborn things; but I'm able to smile about it! (I'll tell you more one day.)

Thanx, in fact, for your thanx for supper - but just to save labour and ink shall we dispense with them in future? I'd prefer to think buying you a spot of grub was now not an occasion formal enough for a formal "thank you".

Next...

I need that "Elle" back desperately fast: it shouldn't have left my hands, I now realise. Could'st leave it outside my door, please.

No American "Vogue" available but I'm bringing a new one back this evening after our somewhat splendid and grand private view of young Pharaoh and his baggage, whither I go at cocktail hour. [The press preview of London's first blockbuster Tutankhamun exhibition.]

Pray also co-ordinate Simunek [my Godfather George Simunek's daughter Kate, an illustrator] *and your photographer earliest possible.* [Illustrations for my next Chandelier feature on beating summer sightseeing fatigue.] *And likewise, make notes as you go along for that "The Guy I was to Meet Was Late" idea.*

Also, I can promise you a further piece for the next "Chandelier", besides.

I can now let you know what there is at this end towards the weekend enterprise.

Heil Fraulein Cellulite!

It was Harold who first taught me the importance of having what journalists call a 'hook' when pitching an idea for an article, both to grab an editor's eye and ensure the subject is topical. One day, I discovered through my local chemist in Marylebone

High Street, that they had begun to import a new kit from France designed to combat cellulite – the stubborn, dimpled excess fat on upper thighs and bottom which can afflict even relatively slim women. Because I had read much about the condition in French magazines and occasionally suffered from it myself, I sent Harold a brief memo – a follow-up to one of my original 'sample articles' I had sent him the previous year – outlining the subject and suggesting an article for *Chandelier*. I stressed it was essentially a scoop, since it had never been written about in the UK and could become a new hot topic.

To my surprise, the memo piqued his interest. To my even greater surprise, it grew on him to the point that he did not commission it for *Chandelier*, deciding instead, after a word with the editor, it would be suitable for the *Femail* section of the *Daily Mail*. So, after my first baby steps for Trusthouse Forte Hotels, this was to be my first article ever in a national daily newspaper.

As with *Chandelier*, he left it to me to come up with the illustrations.

Dear Alix,

Fraulein Cellulite (IT IS GERMAN REALLY, YOU KNOW!).

I "check" on disturbing you as early as 9.30 in the morning by looking to see if your dark blinds are down. [His bathroom and bedroom windows faced mine, and I had mentioned I was an insomniac, a late riser and could only sleep in a totally blacked out room.] *How I envy you the long night's rest. "Alix The Super-Sleeper!"*

Tell me, have you any illustrative material (prepared or in your head) for this cellulite thing? We'll make up our minds this morning on running the thing next week. It could be done with a bit of a flourish, building that word Cellulite up in advance "blurbs".

Pronounce It

"SELL-YOU-LEET"!

A Word that could make a big change in your life...

Harold

Some magazines outside...

*** What a priceless language German is: Page 72 "Stern"*

Diktatur des Orgasmus - *Indeed!*

All I could think of for illustrations to accompany the Cellulite feature was a rather brutal massage technique I had learnt about in France, and even experienced personally while working there. I suggested the moves could be photographed, or sketched, to accompany the article. The idea appealed and he told me to come down to the *Daily Mail* offices and talk to Mac Keene, the founding editor of *Femail*, who would introduce me to someone in the art department.

Nothing prepared me for the excitement of visiting the offices of a national newspaper. Until that day, I had rarely been to Fleet Street; my stomping ground was up the road in Covent Garden. As I got off the bus at Chancery Lane, crossed the busy road and headed down Carmelite Street towards the Thames Embankment, the air crackled with energy, reminding me of midtown Manhattan, as people hurried by purposefully, elbowing their way through the chattering crowd. Northcliffe House, built in 1926 and named after Lord Northcliffe, the founder of the *Daily Mail*, was the headquarters of Associated Newspapers, publishers of the *Evening News* and the *Daily Mail* and occupied an entire block between Carmelite Street and Bouverie Street, bounded by Tudor Street.

To reach the main entrance of the editorial departments meant walking past the building's lower depths, housing the newspapers' printing presses on vast underground floors. At ground level, the loading and dispatch bays were open to the street. Burly men stood by a conveyor belt hauling bundles of the latest edition fresh off the presses, binding and loading them into waiting vans for immediate distribution.

Blocking part of the narrow street, a lorry was parked outside, loaded with giant rolls of newsprint stacked perilously three or four bundles high. Dubbed 'elephants' toilet rolls' by the printers, the job of unloading and hoisting them into the building, with the aid of a small crane, contributed further to the tumult.

I stood transfixed. Until that first trip to the *Daily Mail*, I thought nothing could compare to the heartbeat of Covent Garden and the West End with its own late night magic, long after audiences have gone home and the machinery of theatre is laid bare, stripped of glamour and make-believe. In theatreland, that transformation usually happens when a run ends and a show's sets are 'struck' and removed, or when a ballet or opera company's repertoire changes, and different scenery needs to be installed. At such times, a theatre becomes an industrial site. Dimly lit by single working lights, auditorium, stage, proscenium, scenery, fly tower, lighting grids and battens are starkly exposed. Jagged strains of clattering iron, hammering, and the scraping of metal are interrupted only by an odd shout or profanity from the stage hands.

I was immediately entranced by such behind-the-scenes turmoil when my father first took me backstage at the age of three. I didn't think it could be matched for visual drama, smells, sounds and visceral impact. But now, walking through the industrial zone of 'hot metal' printing, with its cloying odour of ink, molten metal, and the subterranean rumble and clatter of the presses, I experienced the same thrill of being embraced by the roiling guts of a great historic industry.

Upstairs in the editorial offices I found the *Femail* department, a large, noisy space wreathed in cigarette smoke, conversations punctuated by the clacketty-click and ping of typewriters. Mac Keene, a bearded, professorial figure, introduced me to Liz Gill, one of the newspaper's illustrators. We settled at a table to discuss how best to illustrate the Cellulite article. Liz, who was stick thin and, like me, wearing tight jeans, said that since neither of us had cellulite on which I could demonstrate the various massage techniques, could I mime the different actions she should illustrate. Soon, we were convulsed with laughter as I demonstrated how French masseurs used their hands, elbows and forearms to alternately wring, knead, knuckle and roll surplus flesh on the upper thighs as if making bread. Amid good-natured laughter and mock yelps of pain from nearby journalists, Liz soon got the idea and began filling her sketchpad with pictures that turned out to be spot-on.

A few days later, I filed the Cellulite copy, delivering it by hand simply to relive the heady sensation of visiting Fleet Street and the *Daily Mail* offices again. Mac Keene – a man of inscrutable expression and few words – said it would "work well" as a feature, but was unable to give me a date when the article would appear. This, I soon discovered, was common practice in the newspaper world.

I then set about my next commission for *Chandelier*. Being the summer issue, the topic was on *How to Avoid Sightseeing Fatigue*, which presented plenty of scope for me to share my personal experiences as a dedicated walker, and years of visiting foreign cities, trawling historic sites, museums, art galleries and archaeological sites, often in punishing heat.

The subject was close to Harold's heart, since, like me, he hated very hot weather in the city. Hence his tendency to share his woes when the mercury passed 70 Fahrenheit.

Dear Alix,

If you hear the sound of a shotgun in the night (oh yes, I've got the gun!), it will be your trusty friend - a weather suicide. You're probably wise to clear off for a while tho' there's plenty here to be done if you decide not: would you like the "Mail" to hurry up what they owe you - Mac is away on hols?

Now.

There is a provocatively good idea in this "New York

Times" piece – but not just by plagiarising it. Seeing a lot of commercials is called for; cross-questioning advertising agencies; real (not skimped) research – however, all in a fairly interesting, in fact very interesting field.

Maybe tho', anyway, you think this isn't quite "you" yet. We have to "bring you along", have we not?

Spare copy of "Cellulite" I found lying around if you want it. We should get that into the paper pretty soon too – in fact in the next day or two.

Please. I'll want the "NY Times" stuff back in the morning – but I'll talk to you on the telephone.

I have a spare bullet in the barrel if you care to join me...

G'night,

H

PS. Thanx Chandelier stuff. I read that tomorrow, yes?

PPS. Wimbledon. I have tickets for the centre court on the Friday. But when are you back & why should you be interested, anyway, except that it's so pleasant there?

After remaining on hold for several more weeks until a 'suitable' slot came up for publication, the Cellulite feature finally appeared in the *Daily Mail* and Harold was the first to show me that day's first edition.

3.a.m

Here is an early and late edition for you.

It would be arguable that there is some little jinx on you and the "Mail" [My name had been spelt Alex, not Alix], *except for... except for the fact that the people who matter much like the piece! Very much so.*

Any blemishes or virtues it possesses rest not with me as, momentarily, I am punishingly employed on harsher frontiers!

Seriously, I'm glad to see it in: as I say, it sets things up for more, ideas being of the essence.

If spared, I expect to be away until Friday (and I could do without that!). H

Over the next couple of days, I realised the Cellulite article had made something of a splash at the *Daily Mail.* I was entirely unprepared for the large postbag of readers' letters that arrived at the *Femail* office addressed to me. From the remarks of the women writing in, I knew I had touched a nerve. Apparently, until they read my article, not one of them had ever heard the term 'cellulite', though many said they had suffered from it for many years and wanted to know more about its causes and treatment.

And it wasn't only the readers.

A brief typewritten memo, lying outside my door, said it all.

Mac Keene.

Harold Keeble Esq. *12th May, 72*

You might be interested to know that I was informed this morning by the Anti-Cellulite Product Ltd., that the following papers:

Daily Telegraph

Daily Mirror

Sunday Mirror

Sunday Express

Sunday Times

have all been onto the firm concerned, asking why a proper press release was not given to all papers and the series given exclusively to the Daily Mail.

Underneath the memo, Harold's hasty red scribble:

Ve...rry interesting
I made pretty bloody clear it was not a hand-out.
Try to call you from Heathrow. H

5

Dramas, Divas and Defamation

"BITCHY STRITCHY", AS Harold called her, was Elaine Stritch whom, as a teenager, I had so admired in the 1960s musical *Sail Away*: it was one of the shows of that period which convinced me to abandon the idea of a career in ballet and concentrate instead on commercial musical theatre. But much had happened since. Although by the 1970s I was concentrating on straight acting and moving further from 'showbiz' and West End musicals, my contact with that jazzier world had not been entirely severed.

That was the case with Elaine Stritch. After the London run of *Sail Away*, Stritch, who had long been a Broadway name, also became a West End star, famed for her astringent wit, gravelly singing voice and drop-dead timing. In 1972 when she returned to London in Stephen Sondheim's *Company*, she again wowed English audiences as the hard-nosed, heavy drinking Joanne, stopping the show with the coruscating torch song, *Here's to the Ladies who Lunch*, a paean to rich, bored New Yorkers.

Stritch's London success, boosted by the popularity of two

long-running TV sit-coms in which she starred, first with Donald Sinden, and later with Richard Griffiths, led her to settle here. Home was a suite at the Savoy, reputedly secured at a favourable rate so long as she acknowledged and praised her London digs as often as possible in press interviews and TV chat shows.

By this time, two good friends of mine had come to know her well. My flamboyant and glamorous flatmate Nadia, a PA at the National Theatre which was then under the directorship of Sir Laurence Olivier and based at the Old Vic Theatre, had become a close friend of Stritch's, inviting her down to her parents' home in the country and occasionally accompanying her on trips and holidays.

The actress Julia McKenzie, with whom I had shared a dressing room during the long run of *Promises, Promises*, also got to know Stritch from a very different perspective when both were in *Company* at Her Majesty's Theatre. As a heavy drinker – it was only much later when diagnosed with diabetes that she went to AA and admitted being an alcoholic – Stritch could be notoriously difficult to work with.

Donald Sinden, her co-star in the TV series *Two's Company*, admitted publicly that "...her drinking made the first series of the show a trial for me." During the run of *Company*, Julia McKenzie remembered often staying on at the theatre after the curtain came down to accompany her colleague safely back to the Savoy and make sure she went straight to bed without a detour via the American Bar.

Later, Stritch went on to star in a little-known Neil Simon play, *Gingerbread Lady*. The pre-West End tryout of the production at the Theatre Royal Windsor was directed by Julia's husband, Jerry Hjert, a kind, mild-mannered American who became the butt of Stritch's bad temper and bitchiness. Not surprisingly, Elaine and Julia's friendship curdled. And when the play later opened in the West End, the new director was Vivian Matalon, a seasoned old pro evidently better equipped to handle his star's tantrums.

Eventually, when I met Stritch a couple of times with Nadia,

I found her friendly, and was surprised when she revealed a disarmingly childlike innocence behind the brittle facade. She had recently married an American actor, John Bay, whom she met in 1973 when both appeared in a London production of Tennesee Williams' play, *Small Craft Warnings*, and seemed to relax into a newfound calm despite continued drinking. Tragically, that happy period in her life was shattered a few years later when Bay died of a brain tumour.

When Harold discovered my tenuous connection to Stritch, he made sure to pass on any gossip and rumours floating around town, especially via the Fleet Street diary pages. More acerbic, however, was his own appraisal of some of her performances.

Darling Alix,

Why, WHY do these people, whose magic depends upon the preservation of illusion, sit themselves in front of the TV cameras which are so merciless on their deficiencies?

Poor Danny La Rue – a superb artist but a little less than superb on that sad little show: commonplace, predictable, utterly ordinary.

And the wondrous Miss Stritch, confused, self-assertive, incapable of lucid thought, rather ill-mannered and all too manifestly rather squalidly pissed. Why do they actually WANT to fracture the secret ingredient they really possess?

Puzzling.

Please emphasise to your Mama my thanx for the suggestion about coming down on Christmas Day. One possibility has arisen since we last spoke and that is that I might be in Phoenix, Arizona, over that period but it's only about a 60/40 likelihood... oh a bit less than that, I'd say. Midnight in the dry desert air can be very acceptable – but don't you think wisdom about too much travel should prevail? "Boy! Bring forth the chains! Produce the padlock!"

Should I ask doped-up Dennis [an American photographer flatmate of mine] *in for a drink this evening, do you think? I have one idea I could try him on when The Trip of Trips ends (it hadn't ended yesterday!).*

"Love in the Afternoon" - which afternoon? [A new French film I wanted to see.] *And look at our opera list.*

Harold

* * *

AT THAT TIME, an even bigger megawatt star making headlines was Marlene Dietrich, booked to appear in the West End that summer in a one-woman show, accompanied by her musical director, Burt Bacharach. Now in her seventies, she had toured throughout much of the world performing her act, in which she sang standard ballads as well as the songs she made famous in her youth, including *Lili Marlene*, *They Call me Naughty Lola* and *Falling In love Again*. She was signed up to make a videotaped version of her stage show, for transmission on New Year's Day 1973 on BBC TV and a fortnight later on CBS in the USA. Rehearsals and filming were scheduled for late November at London's New Theatre, allowing plenty of time for Dietrich to give interviews and make promotional appearances in the week leading up to the UK and US broadcasts.

Harold found himself caught up in securing an exclusive *Daily Mail* interview with Dietrich to promote the show and was delighted to have tracked down exactly the right high-profile show business interviewer – himself a celebrity in the USA – to get a different angle on the ageing star.

Darling Alix

Do you know the American writer Rex Reed - or at least his work? I had lunch with him today (Very amusing. He's a civilised American) and he's done us a somewhat unconventional Dietrich interview.

I have seen a preview of the show. Sad, I thought. Suddenly, suddenly... it's gone! All that you see now (well nearly) is the creaking mechanics: the goldfish-gaping mouth, the agonising predictability, the terrifying pretence that it's magic when the reality is stale, stale STALE... a performance for men with poor prostates.

No good, no good at all, the big blow-up backcloth (like a Hitler rally); no good that out-of-date timing; no good at all the fur wrap which made her look like Mrs Five-by-Five; no good the frenziedly organised floral fusillades. Corpseville!

Have you read "Jonathan Livingstone Seagull"? The stubborn fact is that this little book has been No 1 on the US best-seller list for thirty-three weeks.

This record of "Firebird" – it's yours, I think.

Love

HAROLD

With these comments fresh in my mind, I watched the TV show two days later. Initially surprised at his excoriating remarks, I saw he was bang on the nail. I had seen Dietrich give a midnight matinee performance in Edinburgh in the 1960s and even then, her act struck me as outdated although, as a gay icon, she was obviously trading on the high camp elements of her earlier film roles. Now, over a decade later, her fan base increasingly vociferous and adoring, the ageing Priestess of High Camp continued to give them more of what they wanted. By now, the creaking machinery Harold so abhorred was simply embarrassing.

But, more drama was to come.

8 am.

Dearest Alix,

An early emergency call – but I expect to be back for

some sleep, I hope, around lunchtime; and I'll ring you then.

The enclosed may engage your passing interest! It's really quite astonishing stuff from Dietrich.

It seems one's reaction was right, despite the unqualified adoration of Nadia. [My ex-flatmate, a big fan of Dietrich's, had left the National Theatre and was working as a model, with Joanna Lumley, for the fashion designer Jean Muir and created a tribute act, complete with blonde wig and glitter gown, miming to a soundtrack of Dietrich's songs.]

I got Rex Reed to see The Great Glamour-Frau again and, boy, did she burn 'em up! The stuff I've sub-edited out is quite interesting too. I think it will all cause a bit of a hullabaloo.

Hang on to it, will you please?

How about "Carmen" on Jan 30? (I'm not - well hardly!!! - suggesting we don't meet until then.) But I've discovered the best place to sit in that vast theatre. [Opera House, Covent Garden.] *It is Box M: two seats and one spare for your belongings and to ease the claustrophobia.*

Love, H

PS. Don't "bait" Nadia tho, will you? Her respect and love for middle-aged and very old ladies is sweet, absolutely sweet!

The more I regaled Harold with 'inside information' – via mutual friends – about Marlene Dietrich, the more he relished me spilling the beans. The most colourful secrets I discovered about her came from a dapper and gregarious Englishman, Bernard – 'BJ' – Hall, who used to stay on and off in my flat when he was in town. BJ, whom I had met through Nadia, was a former actor, dancer, fitness teacher and choreographer who, for many years, had worked as Marlene Dietrich's private secretary, personal trainer, dresser and general factotum.

Aged in his late forties, BJ, also a good friend of Elaine Stritch, split his time – when not on tour with Dietrich – flitting between her Right Bank Paris apartment at 48 Avenue Montaigne, and his own small Left Bank studio, pitching up occasionally in London where he lodged with one of his many friends, including me or Nadia, who was now living opposite Portman Mansions in a block above Baker Street Station.

The degree of intimacy between BJ and "the German Hausfrau" as he called her, due to her habit of pulling on the Marigolds and scrubbing floors on her hands and knees, was breathtaking. So was his indiscretion. Many people would be tempted to dismiss his 'backstage secrets' as the product of a vivid imagination, but I knew better. It turned out that their relationship was very close indeed and, as I got to know him better, I realised he had become a true intimate of hers, as probably only a gay man can.

He showed me photos of the two of them together on various trips and let me read her letters from Paris, accompanied by press cuttings, their margins filled with caustic remarks scribbled in a flamboyant hand with red or green fibre-tip pen – not unlike Harold's memos. There was also genuine affection between the two. When BJ stayed with me for several weeks during the 'winter of discontent' and the three-day week, with its power cuts, panic buying and much publicised food shortages, food parcels would arrive from Paris containing packet soups, tea bags, coffee and much else, with strict instructions from Dietrich that he must eat enough and stay healthy.

When I asked what she looked like off stage and at home, his 'warts and all' description shattered the myth of the world's perennially youthful 'glamorous grandmother'. It wasn't a pretty picture. Beneath the sleekly coiffed blonde hair – in fact a custom-made wig from the leading theatrical firm, Wig Creations – her hair was sparse, grey and unkempt. He described her face, devoid of makeup, as crumpled and wrinkly as "a Cox's orange pippin". Before stage shows and TV appearances, BJ would help fashion the flawlessly smooth public mask by glueing strips of tape to the loose skin at her temples and behind the earlobes, pulling the tapes up and knotting them at the top of her scalp before fitting the wig.

But surely a surgical face lift would be more effective and less bother?

Apparently not, according to BJ. She always dismissed the idea as too dangerous, revealing an innate black humour.

Mimicking her low voice and German accent, he told me, "She always said to me, "Dahling, with my luck, the surgeon vood be a Naaa-zi and ze whole operation vood end up a disaaaster!""

As for the notorious streamlined silhouette beneath the clinging, semi-transparent gown, that too was a feat of artifice. Dietrich's three hours of preparation for any public appearance began with the fitting of a pink latex full-body corset which vacuum-packed her flesh from crotch to neckline. The nude-look 'body double' had to be pulled as tight as possible and hooked into place before she stepped into a sheer, gauzy, jewelled evening gown. To hide the edge of the latex collar – which disguised her crepey neck – she covered the join with a wide diamanté choker.

If I needed more proof that BJ's intimacy with Dietrich wasn't a gay man's fantasy, it came one Sunday afternoon when he was staying with me and had gone on a weekend bender, hitting the bottle non-stop between Friday lunchtime and Monday morning. I had only recently discovered he was an alcoholic, albeit with often long periods of behaving lucidly and normally and drinking only moderately. As he lay senseless, surrounded by empty wine bottles, upstairs in my tiny attic room, the phone rang.

I instantly recognised the low, throaty German accent, the courteous and measured tone, asking politely if she could please speak to Mr Bernard Hall. Apologising that he was unavailable and that I couldn't call him as he was still sleeping soundly, she reacted within a nano-second. Further explanation was unnecessary.

"Oh dear. He is still in bed?"

I muttered in assent.

"So he is drinking again."

It was a statement, not a question.

"Then I suppose it is really bad this time," she sighed, with a mixture of sympathy and longsuffering recognition.

"I don't know why this happens ov-ah and ov-ah again. I sent him to a clinic in Switzerland once, I paid for one of the finest alcohol rehabilitation programmes. He was fine for a while, but it didn't laaahst. I just don't understand why he does it. Do you?"

I confessed I had no idea.

"With Hemingway" – [reputedly one of Dietrich's lovers] – "it used to be because of some wooooman. Or depression. Errol Flynn had the same problem. But with Bernard I never know."

By now, it was blindingly obvious that the two were on the most intimate terms and that she was genuinely fond of him, concerned for his welfare yet dismayed by his self-destructiveness. We chatted for a few more minutes and she advised me to leave him alone to sleep it off, but make sure to remove any alcohol lying around which he might be tempted to consume.

Her parting shot: "And don't let his friends come to visit him with bottles."

When I told Harold the story, he listened glumly and then testily gave his own verdict on the diva. Marlene Dietrich had just become *persona non grata* to him and the entire *Daily Mail* management and editorial teams, who now faced a massive libel action because of her indiscretions during the Rex Reed interview – which Harold had personally set up. During the interview, Dietrich let rip, presumably because she knew Reed well, and decided to trash the TV show, accusing the production team of unprofessionalism, slamming the recording as technically inept.

When asked how she rated the TV programme, she dismissed it witheringly as a mediocre version of her original stage show. Above all, she made it clear that she loathed the medium of TV.

"The conditions were very difficult," she confided to Reed. "They work you to death. I started out at 4 o'clock and at 2.30 in the morning I was still standing there. We had two days, we should have taken a week." The implication was obvious: the show was made on the cheap.

She may have had a point. With rehearsal time so severely limited, she still gave two full performances of her stage act on two consecutive days in front of an invited black-tie audience at the New Theatre. After the shows were taped, with interruptions for different cut-away audience shots, they went on to film retakes of her most famous songs, against a black backcloth. This allowed the director to create a split screen, one side featuring Dietrich's present performance, the other side displaying a montage of black and white stills from her old films.

She clearly hated the process. "You can't do exactly what you want to do. This is on tape and tape is a very cruel thing. It isn't like film. Film has depth and dimension but tape has not, so you look flat. You can't control it. A small screen is really frustrating."

BJ had told me about Dietrich's fanatical perfectionism during rehearsals for her stage shows, in particular her extensive knowledge of stage and screen lighting and camera angles – acquired through years of working with the finest film directors like Von Sternberg, Billy Wilder and Orson Welles. So I sympathised with her very real frustration with the fast-paced process of TV and an unforgiving medium like videotape. She was, after all, from another era. "I like live shows. I like to see live performances. TV is wonderful for people who are lonesome or ill."

When the interview came out in the *Daily Mail*, Harold's prediction that it would cause "a bit of a hullabaloo" proved a classic understatement. Hours after the first edition rolled off the presses, the TV show's producer, Alexander H. Cohen, one of Broadway's leading impresarios who had produced many of Dietrich's previous world tours, Broadway and West End shows, started a libel action against the newspaper and demanded $500,000 in damages. Cohen saw her remarks as both a personal betrayal and an affront to his professional reputation. Denouncing her treachery, he cancelled all the upcoming stage shows he had organised for her that coming year and refused ever to work with her again.

"Over the six years when she did two one-woman shows in New York and went on tour, I showed up in every city to be of help," Cohen raged to a US newspaper. "The way that she treated me was no way to treat a friend. I have no quarrel with the press – it is only with her highness."

Cohen was incandescent at the potential financial damage from Dietrich's outburst. In the USA, the chief sponsor of her show on CBS was the corporate giant Kraft Foods – and it was feared that Kraft might withdraw their sponsorship or reduce it. Another fallout from Rex Reed's interview was that Cohen claimed he had lost some lucrative sales in Europe.

Although Cohen's action against the *Daily Mail* in the UK was settled out of court for an undisclosed sum, in the US the case dragged on for several years – with Dietrich bringing a separate claim against Cohen for $100,000, allegedly the unpaid final instalment of part of her $250,000 contract – reportedly the highest TV fee ever paid at that time to a solo performer. Writs flew back and forth across the Atlantic and finally, after four years of claims and counterclaims, in 1977 the case was dropped after Dietrich failed to attend court in New York due to illness. What many people didn't know was that by that time, her career was over. During an appearance in Sydney in 1976, she broke her thigh in a fall onstage and never gave another performance.

It always surprised me how much of a kick Harold got from show business gossip as well as from the foibles and narcissism of some of the big names he dealt with. Was there still something starry-eyed about the native Yorkshireman, born in Dewsbury, raised in Leeds, who came to London and straight into Fleet Street in his twenties, with little intervening cosmopolitan input? Or was it because, as he told me, he often worked in the heavyweight sections of the newspaper, politics, current affairs, the business pages, that celebrity tales came as a welcome light relief? I believe it was a mixture of both.

Dearest Alix,

We move jerkily – indeed slip backwards in some ways.

a) You were right about the first item on the World Theatre Season being one week only (the booking response for the whole season has been tremendous). However, the seats are being changed either for the Tuesday of that week or the Friday and they'll ring me at 5 o'clock and let me know.

b) I enclose tickets for the other evening. Bergman's "Wild Duck".

c) Signore Visconti (like others we know) is a frenzied last-minute cutter! So much so that even the New York premiere itself has been postponed, which must be causing some inconvenience. Hence the promised print due here will not be due here this week – probably not for two more weeks. Nevertheless, we are to meet the mad 'Ludwig' when he does arrive, as we're doing a special advance story on the film.

d) If – not sure I can but if – I go to the enclosed Snowdon [an exhibition of his friend Lord Snowdon's latest photographs] *thing, will you honour me with your company? I have been to Olympia this morning with Tony and it's really even a better show than Cologne.*

e) Here is a copy of "Jumpers"! So you may relish the prose.

f) I look forward to meeting up this evening at 8.15 (but, as you know, my medic checks me in at 10.30!).

I imagine the general air transport/customs balls-up is fortunately detaining Bernard in the capital here.

Love

Harold

PS: Did they hitch Stritch? [a reference to Elaine Stritch's marriage to the actor John Bay].

6

Master of the Dark Arts

THE BETTER I got to know him, the more I found Harold to be the most self-deprecating person I had ever met. Notably, he once casually let slip that he was awarded an OBE after the war, insisting that in terms of personal distinction it really "meant nothing", citing the old joke that OBE stood for "other buggers' efforts". When I found his name listed in the London phone book and asked why he wasn't ex-directory, he retorted that trying to hide one's contact details was "the ultimate affectation".

On another occasion, he told me his UK bank had recently made an unfortunate mistake and wrongly frozen his account, leaving him without access to money. Quite by chance, he remembered that on a trip to America long ago, he had opened an account with the Wells Fargo Bank in the US, and realised he could use it to draw funds for unexpected emergencies – a resource he put down to "the unacceptable face of privilege".

What he lacked in vanity or ego, he more than made up for with a keen sense of the ridiculous, a delightful quality which furnished many of his stories and general gossip.

Dear Alix,

Just got your note – and very glad to: thought I'd lost touch with my fashion consultant and very good friend! Oh Christ, Christmas! Yes, yes indeed – the conspiracy ensnares you, dodge it as you will. I'd hoped to talk you into dinner or something, but I suppose now the familiar phrase "after Christmas" pops up.

Tonight (in some ways, alas,) I'm having dinner with Michael Redgrave at the Daubenys – thank God just six of us! – but I'd be back by just after eleven and you don't always go to bed that early! I'm going to try and get back to the flat for an hour before going to Chester Square (so maybe then?) but if I'm, as likely, caught at the office, I'll telephone you.

You might like to read the enclosed [a Daily Mail article] *– result of a most extraordinary episode yesterday. Off-chance request to Richard Burton and within 24 hours he dictated this whole thing in to the "Daily Mail" telephone operators. He then spent another 45 minutes dictating corrections and, when appreciation was expressed, said: "Well, please tell my wife you think it's good: here she is."*

From someone who I suppose earns (say) £5,000 a day... an odd, unexpected gesture.

H

* * *

I ALWAYS ASSUMED Harold was awarded an OBE for his services to journalism, principally the many years he spent working alongside the legendary reforming editor Arthur Christiansen, in transforming the image and the circulation of the *Daily Express* during the era of Lord Beaverbrook. But I was wrong. Because he never spoke about his experiences during WWII, I had to winkle out tiny nuggets of information from various books, newspapers and some reminiscences of his wartime colleagues.

The truth he sought to hide – most likely because even in the 1970s he was still strictly bound by the Official Secrets Act – turned out to be far more significant. And, as so often in his life, the reality was both colourful and partly shrouded in mystery, involving the British Secret Services, and the dissemination of so-called 'Black Propaganda' against Nazi Germany and occupied Europe during the Second World War. Not for the first time did it occur to me how much of his background resembled the plot of a 1940s spy thriller.

As a young man in his twenties, Harold had begun working at the *Daily Express* in the mid 1930s, when he met an older *Express* journalist who was rapidly gaining a reputation as a 'colossus' of foreign correspondents. Sefton Delmer, known by all as 'Tom', an imposing six foot four, was a shambling bear of a man, brilliant, gregarious, and larger than life – exactly Harold's type of man. The two soon became friends, as well as colleagues.

Born in Berlin in 1904, Sefton Delmer, the son of an Australian professor of English at Berlin University, was first educated in Berlin while also becoming fluent in English. After the end of the First World War, the family emigrated to England and he completed his education at St Pauls and Lincoln College Oxford, becoming a freelance journalist until he was hired by the *Daily Express* to head the newspaper's new Berlin office in 1928.

Delmer's native language and immersion in German culture and history gave him a massive advantage over other English correspondents when he began to cover Hitler's early political activities and rise to power. As he came to know many key members of the Nazi Party, he reported on Germany's 1932 election, travelled with Hitler in his private aeroplane on his campaign journeys and became the first journalist to land an interview with Hitler for a British newspaper.

That interview was topped by his biggest scoop, in early 1933, when he witnessed the burning of the Reichstag, with Hitler at his side saying to him: "Let us pray to God this is the work of the communists. You are witnessing the beginning of a great new epoch in German history, Herr Delmer. This fire is the beginning," then proceeding to outline his plan for the future.

After the conflagration, when Delmer phoned his copy through to the *Daily Express* copy-takers, the sub-editors, typically more concerned with factual accuracy than the drama of the story, wanted to know above all how many fire engines had been sent in to tackle the blaze.

Later, Delmer reported on the Spanish civil war, became head of the *Daily Express* Paris bureau and returned to Britain after the outbreak of the Second World War to work for BBC Radio in their German department. As the war progressed, he decided he could no longer simply report on Germany's activities but had to take an active role against the Nazis.

However, when he applied for intelligence work he hit a brick wall. Although he talked to several of his friends who had joined the Secret Services, including cartoonist Osbert Lancaster, author Ian Fleming and Leonard Ingrams (father of Richard Ingrams, co-founder of Private Eye) about undertaking undercover work, his first application was turned down. Given his acquaintance with Hitler and top members of the Nazi Party during his early career, the British authorities, perhaps understandably, at first suspected he might be a Nazi agent.

Following a meticulous background check, Delmer finally got security clearance and was invited by Leonard Ingrams, then at the Political Warfare Executive (PWE), and Ian Fleming, working in naval intelligence, to join the clandestine Special Operations Executive (SOE) at Woburn. This new secret department of the British Foreign Office specialised in that darkest of the dark arts, psychological warfare, and Delmer was recruited to set up a clandestine broadcasting unit to produce German language radio programmes. His remit was to broadcast 'black propaganda' to confuse, mislead and demoralise the Germans throughout the continent of Europe. The new radio station was based in a large, requisitioned house in Milton Bryan, Buckinghamshire not far from the code-breaking activities of Bletchley Park.

For the next four years, Delmer was in his element. From May 1941, 'black radio' went on air live every day and was broadcast only in German, by native German speakers with instantly recognisable regional accents. It therefore gave every impression of coming directly from inside Germany. The programmes reached everyone from Nazi officers and military troops, to ordinary Germans who believed they had tuned into an unofficial German pirate station and it soon became compulsive listening compared to the bland, censored official radio offerings from the Third Reich.

The appeal lay in its scope and sometimes shocking content. Although listeners would hear the latest German news including reports from the front line, an added attraction was the inclusion of popular music, risqué comedians and satirical sketches, interspersed with salacious and disturbing rumours, invented gossip – all fabricated by Delmer's team in Buckinghamshire. The on-air ragings and rantings of ordinary German citizens who, while loyal to the Führer, disapproved of the alleged depravity, corruption and privileges of the Nazi elite, was another inspired piece of propaganda.

One popular commentator, known only as 'Der Chef', (The Chief), was a curmudgeonly old Prussian, a foul-mouthed racist and antisemite with a guttural Berlin accent: Der Chef was pro-Hitler but anti SS, and denounced individual Nazi functionaries in vulgar, expletive-laden language. In fact, Der Chef was acted by Paul Saunders, a young German writer from Berlin who fled Germany in 1933 and settled in Britain. Saunders was one of several Germans who made up Delmer's nucleus of actors.

None of the listeners could ever have guessed this nightly diversion came from a small studio in Milton Bryan, every item selected, verified and delivered by Delmer and his team. That team, which continued to expand, consisted of a ramshackle group of radio engineers, German refugees, prisoners of war, as well as emigré actors, academics and writers who had fled Nazi Germany before 1939.

The factual accuracy of each broadcast was paramount, and the studio relied heavily on its own record library and intelligence files since the objective was to deliver news reports and talks that were wholly correct and therefore entirely plausible to German ears. To that end, Delmer insisted the material must be eighty percent accurate; the other twenty percent was fake news, surreptitiously smuggled into the broadcast to sow the seeds of dissatisfaction, doubt and confusion in the minds of Germans at every level.

Eventually, in early 1944, with plans in preparation for the Allied invasion of Europe, Delmer, now Director of Special Operations, decided to add a newspaper to their arsenal of black propaganda. *Nachrichten für die Truppe* (News for the Troops), which Delmer began planning eighteen months earlier, would contain the same 80/20 percentage of factually correct reportage alongside slanted or fake news. By then, his team had recruited more British, American and exiled German writers, sub-editors, secretaries, illustrators and photographers, all the staff necessary to produce a daily newspaper.

As a joint Anglo-American venture, this was the first Allied newspaper aimed specifically at German forces, and Delmer oversaw the editorial content, wrote much of the material and cheered on his staff. Every night, he and his assistants put the paper together from the news and talks featured on one of their current radio programmes, *Soldatensender*: this recycled material was sub-edited and rewritten for print.

The features editor called in to supervise the typography, editing and layout was Delmer's former *Daily Express* colleague Harold Keeble, who, at thirty-three, was already recognised for his flair and originality as a design and layout expert. Long before *Nachrichten* was launched, Harold was sent by the SOE to America on several research trips to consult – and where possible hire – experts in newspaper design, typography and the advertising business, to ensure that *Nachrichten* appeared to German eyes as professional and realistically home-grown as possible.

Back in England, Harold took charge of a team of American and English artists, compositors and printers, who designed and laid out *Nachrichten für die Truppe* at Marylands, another large, requisitioned house near Woburn. His role in delivering false information to the enemy represented just one key element in an intricate operation run by multinational journalists, writers and illustrators, master forgers, actors and secret service agents, all of whom happened to be in the right place at the right time.

For light relief, the paper even included sports results, cartoons – including the work of Osbert Lancaster – and pin-ups. Both Delmer and Keeble were perfectionists, sticklers for detail and worked tirelessly to publish a perfect dummy issue of *Nachrichten* before its proper launch. The first edition of the paper appeared on April 25th 1944, with an initial run of 200,000 copies assembled and printed by a Luton-based publisher which produced the local *Luton News*. The finished product was loaded into so-called 'leaflet bombs' for collection by the men of the British Night Leaflet Squadron, who deposited them at a designated airfield to be dropped over Germany and occupied Europe during the course of the night.

Soon, daily production of *Nachrichten für die Truppe* topped one million. Under Delmer and Harold's leadership, the team's capacity for high-speed work and split-second decision-making during fast-changing events was crucial in the last year of the war. On 6th June, D Day, the German news agency transmitted an emergency news alert concerning the invasion and this was picked up in the afternoon by a transcriber at Milton Bryan. That evening, the radio team aired the news on *Soldatensender* and Delmer, knowing the next edition of *Nachrichten* must carry these latest updates, drove at high speed to Marylands to join Harold in putting together a new front page for the newspaper. The rest of the team were called in at 3.30am and by 10am, 800,000 copies of the paper rolled off the presses, with full coverage of the D-Day story.

Inevitably, the men and women working with Delmer, and those based at Marylands with Harold, formed close-knit communities under conditions of the highest secrecy. With two such ebullient men at the helm, the atmosphere at each centre was one of loyal dedication leavened with high-spirited bonhomie. Following the fall of Calais, the black radio programme *Soldatensender Calais* went off the air for good on April 14th 1945. To celebrate, Delmer shaved off the beard he had grown since 1941, and gave a party in the canteen at Milton Bryan. Under relaxed security, for the first time in the war staff from there and Marylands were allowed to socialise together.

After the surrender of Germany on May 7th 1945, the last issue of *Nachrichten für die Truppe* was put to bed and this time Harold held a celebration party in the print shop at Marylands. The high point of the evening was John Gibb, the editor of the *Luton News* who had contributed so much to getting *Nachrichten* up and running, arriving at the festivities wearing a suit printed with all the front pages of the newspaper. In total, almost 160 million copies of *Nachrichten* had been printed. Like the radio broadcasts from Milton Bryan, it was recognised that the black propaganda Delmer and Harold had so skilfully rolled out through the last years of the war, had contributed significantly to the enemy's last period of confusion, chaos and final collapse.

Soon after VE Day, Delmer and some of his team moved back to London to begin work on the reconstruction of press and radio services in Germany's British Occupied Zone. Harold followed suit, eager to play a part and travelled to Cologne, now under American occupation, to help rebuild some of the newspaper presses destroyed by the Allies.

He knew that Cologne had played a pivotal role in the early history of newspapers in the 19th Century, long before the creation of a unified Germany. In 1822, the owner of *Kölnische Zeitung* newspaper, Joseph Du Mont, installed the first steam press in the country, making his newspaper one of the bestselling publications throughout the1800s and early1900s. More importantly, throughout its history, the *Kölnische Zeitung* remained Germany's foremost democratic and liberal newspapers – even as the spectre of Nazism cast its infernal shadow over Europe.

After 1945, Harold's wartime experiences and contacts in the Secret Service proved invaluable when he returned to newspaper work. Always on the lookout for controversial books to serialise in the newspaper, as Associate Editor of the *Daily Express,* he bought the pre-publication rights to a true story by Ewen Montagu, a naval intelligence officer, revealing the background of an audacious secret WWII operation. There was one problem: the book had no title. The plot, codenamed *Operation Mincemeat*, was masterminded by Montagu, and involved the RAF dropping a dead man's body in undergrowth inside enemy lines to deceive the Germans about the allied invasion of Sicily in 1943.

After trawling hospital mortuaries, secret agents found the corpse of an unnamed middle-aged vagrant, kitted him out in the uniform of a Royal Marine Officer, and stuffed his pockets with false ID papers, personal photographs and love letters from his 'girlfriend' to further convince the Germans. Crucially, official government documents were planted on the body which falsely identified Greece, not Sicily, as the location of the upcoming allied invasion. Falling straight into the trap, the Germans headed for Greece while the allies successfully landed in Sicily. Ewen Montagu, who had already resumed his peacetime career as a judge, was unable to come up with a title – but within minutes Harold nailed it. *The Man Who Never Was* went on to become a world bestseller and a popular film, spawning numbers of subsequent books and dramatisations, even a 2023 musical of the story.

As the 1950s progressed, it was no coincidence that Harold was the first newspaper editor to spot the potential of another series of spy thrillers. Having first got to know Ian Fleming during the war, when the writer was in charge of Royal Navy Intelligence and both men worked under the aegis of the SOE, Harold pounced instantly on pre-publication hype for *Dr No*, the first of the James Bond novels. He secured serialisation rights to the book, and to all subsequent 007 thrillers, helping the books become roaring bestsellers. More significantly, given

Harold's eminence on Fleet Street, through the 1950s and 1960s these lavish, specially illustrated extracts of the Bond novels, and of other bestselling thriller writers, added thousands to the *Daily Express* readership and to the coffers of Beaverbrook Newspapers.

7

Sell The Sizzle, Not The Steak

It was just over a year since Harold asked me to write for *Chandelier* and helped get my first article into the *Daily Mail*. Being commissioned to write those pieces, then seeing them in print, worked wonders for my confidence and prompted me to spread my wings further. It was, of course, that intoxicating liminal period when, driven by passion, a beginner has no idea how little they know about a profession. So, with the blind self-belief born of naiveté and inexperience, I set my sights on *Vogue* despite having no contacts there. What was there to lose? Given nobody knew my name and I had no track record or professional reputation, rejection would damage nothing more consequential than my ego. But because British *Vogue* was already crammed with beauty and style features covered by staff writers, I had to find a gap in the market.

Once again, I turned for inspiration to French and German magazines, which covered women's health from a medical and popular science angle. Popular topics ranged from premenstrual tension, the menopause, natural versus 'medicalised' childbirth, to newly popular 'holistic' healthcare including acupuncture of the ear, foot reflexology and shiatsu. With no idea who to approach at Condé Nast with my proposals, I phoned their switchboard and was given the name of *Vogue's* associate editor, Barbara Timms, who dealt with freelance contributions.

To my astonishment, once I began pitching my ideas, which I delivered with a covering letter by hand to Vogue House in Hanover Square, not only did Barbara Timms reply to my letters, she also ended up commissioning almost all the features I suggested. To my even greater surprise, the articles were published with few changes or cuts and each feature was given generous space, a bold title and a prominent by-line.

Although I put my early *Vogue* commissions down to beginner's luck, I recognised that Harold had taught me one of the most valuable, yet overlooked, skills of journalism: salesmanship. When it came to the art of the pitch, Harold was a past master. That included the succinct, one-sentence 'elevator pitch'; so-called in the United States because you had to sell an idea to an editor in the time it took to travel between several floors in an office building. Through him, I learnt another key strategy borrowed from all spheres of American commerce and marketing. 'Sell the Sizzle, not the Steak' meant talking up the hype and excitement swirling around a product, before zeroing in on the product itself. The challenge lay in so impressing an editor with one's enthusiasm that they commissioned the story. More and more, I learnt that securing a commission was an art in itself and could be as satisfying as getting an editor's approval – sometimes coming a close second to the thrill of seeing one's article in print.

Of course I was hugely gratified by Harold's largely positive responses to my 'outside' work.

Dear young Miss K,

First class! Absolutely excellent. Informative. Lots of conviction. Relaxed. Expressed with <u>authority</u> – neatly broken with that familiar (award winning) chuckle which *dissolves any chance of drifting towards the pompous, which the subject tends to engender. Right? Talk to you later if, IF I am near a "convenient" telephone.*

There's a treasure – really a treasure of writing – outside your door. Something unexcelled in unpleasantness and skill: I've told Dempster [Nigel Dempster, the Daily Mail's gossip columnist] *he's only on the nursery slopes of nastiness. Capote. Read it slowly.*

Again, sincere "congratters". H

My dream was also to write for the *Guardian*, whose women's pages represented the pinnacle of top quality, informative and sociologically aware writing on women's 'issues'. All serious aspiring journalists, women or men, wanted to write for the *Guardian* – not for the money, which was then, as it is now, paltry, but for the prestige and respect it generated among fellow writers and commissioning editors. As I learned from pitching to the *Daily Mail* and *Vogue*, coming up with original, relatively unknown topics, or approaching familiar subjects from an unusual angle, was the key to getting commissioned. It was also one of Harold's favourite mantras.

Alix m'love,

Momentarily a bit pushed.

Useful magazine haul outside though.

Pray press on!

Originality.

Variety.

Compactness of language.

Also keep a constantly alert eye above all for the isolated picture which has some meaningful place and impact in these "FEMAIL" pages: we have an enormous (and unfulfilled) hunger for pictures of Stop-I-Must-Look quality. Devour the magazines: not just the obvious ones – the slanted, tilted, off-beat ones, from "Ebony" to "Village Voice", to "Gynaecology", to "New York", etc. Read incessantly. Reading something on the spot is somehow quite different from reading the same thing thousands of miles away. In my view, the best writing, for sheer precision of language, are the political editorials in the opening Notes of the "New Yorker".

Love H

By now, experience had taught me that devouring magazines and newspapers, especially foreign ones, could lead to a treasure trove of ideas. A newer concept to me – until I witnessed the extent of Harold's passion for arresting pictures and photographs – was the importance of sharpening one's visual sense. He had a way of identifying the inherent mood and message within a single photograph, capturing its essence and building it into a story. It was the visual equivalent of selling the sizzle and his excitement at getting the 'right' pictures around which to build a feature was infectious.

Such discoveries inspired great glee. He became a small boy in a sweet shop, as when he shoved a two-foot-square sheet of tracing paper through my letterbox one morning, on which he had scrawled a rough experimental layout of a double page feature for the *Daily Mail*. It was about a long drawn-out New York lawsuit brought by Jackie Onassis against the American *paparazzo,* Ron Galella, for harassment and invasion of privacy. Harold's chosen title, *WHY SO ANGRY, JACKIE?* in bold two-inch handwritten capitals, was sub-headed: *He may haunt you, but the man you're battling with in court makes you look a terrific 42.* Dominating the article was an arresting picture of Jackie Onassis with windswept hair, whom Galella had caught unaware as she turned her head to look behind her. Several other shots of her studded the feature.

When Harold and I discussed the case a few days previously,

I mentioned how flattering Galella's photos were, compared with how so many 'wolf pack' photographers made their unsuspecting celebrities, especially women, look their worst. It was almost as if the man hounding Jackie Onassis was in love with her.

And in a way he was. Ron Galella, who was among the world's leading hotshot *paparazzi,* famed for his punch-ups with male film celebrities including Marlon Brando and Warren Beatty, had been stalking Jackie Onassis for over a year – even while she holidayed in Greece. He made a fortune selling his photos of her, and her children, to various international publications and obviously lay in wait for his quarry, plotting the best angles from which to shoot. He had a knack of snapping her fast before she could see him and react. In the end, Onassis won the lawsuit and the judge issued an injunction against Galella, ordering him to go no closer to her than fifty yards, and seventy-five yards to her children.

In the top left corner of Harold's Onassis v. Galella feature layout, he had scrawled:

Miss Kirsta:

So the lady influences our thinking...

Result of your comments t'other evening, I bought those pictures (pretty pricey too, alas!) as I thought you had quite a woman's view on them.

Repeat that: Newspapers need women not just to write about clothes! Need 'em around: bright ones.

See too little of you and not just for reasons mentioned above solely.

H

* * *

After a couple of rejections from the *Guardian*, I finally landed the first of several *Guardian* commissions from the women's page editor, Angela Neustatter. Although the articles were little more than 600 to 800 words, they did cover diverse areas. As my friends latched on to the fact that I was constantly on the lookout for new things to write about, they started coming up with ideas and stories they had seen and heard. This was how I found out about an intriguing new 'cantilevered' bra, designed according to torque-twist engineering principles which apparently made it unique – although the idea reminded me a bit of the bra designed by an aeronautics engineer in the 1940s, which the publishing magnate Howard Hughes commissioned for the Hollywood star, Lana Turner.

I was introduced to the cantilevered bra by Sally Farmiloe, a very pretty 'glamour' model and actress who, in the 1950s, would have been dubbed a 'glamour puss' and signed up as a Rank starlet. Sally, a hardworking and go-getting woman with multiple skills and impressive media and social contacts, was doing PR for various health, beauty, and fashion products and asked me if I wanted to write about the bra, which I did for the *Guardian*.

When some of my dancer friends began raving about a new resistance-based exercise system imported from the United States called Pilates, after its inventor Joseph Pilates, I went off to try it at a small studio on Euston Road and became fanatically devoted to Pilates for the rest of my life. The Body Control Studio in Euston Road was run by Alan Herdman, a genial, empathetic man and superb teacher, who had recently brought the Pilates system to the UK and adapted parts of it to meet the rehabilitation needs of injured dancers as well as more seriously disabled men and women.

Whereas the intricate system of pulleys, springs, weights and push-me-pull-you machinery of Pilates is today a familiar sight in many gyms and exercise studios, in the 1970s it was regarded as a new-fangled method of near torture only suited to the stoicism and iron strength of professional dancers and athletes. This made Alan Herdman the leading rehabilitation specialist for dancers, from the Royal Ballet to the casts of West End musicals.

The Pilates system seemed so original and brilliantly thought out, with extensive powers to help women especially achieve a slimmer, stronger, more streamlined body, that I had no trouble in persuading *Vogue* to run a feature on its potential for physical transformation. Little did I realise that the article was in fact a scoop – I later discovered my piece was the first feature about Pilates in the UK.

It took an artist of the calibre of Gillian Lynne, who made her name and her fortune as the choreographer of *Cats*, to comment, "I would have been a different dancer and choreographer if I had been lucky enough to do Pilates earlier in life", for Pilates to take off as a popular form of physical improvement. Alan Herdman soon relocated to a large studio in Marylebone and became the principal trainer of scores of new teachers who helped spread the popularity of Pilates classes for fitness enthusiasts throughout the UK.

Harold's thumbs-up on this piece ran to a couple of sentences, unusually, since his comments on my work, whether good or bad, tended to be brief.

MEMO

From Harold Keeble

To Miss Alexandra Kirsta

I am immensely impressed with the lead-in on the "Vogue" piece. You may not know it, but it marks a real advance on anything I've seen from you heretofore. The whole piece in fact.

One or two sentences I stumbled on – very minor things tho'.

If you have a copy of this, keep it by you. I'd like David English to read it without knowing where it came from. That is if you are agreeable.

And what date did the "Guardian" stuff appear, please?

Wasn't that good last night! [We had been to see the Royal Ballet at Covent Garden.] *Even Mrs Keeble's philistine son, Harold, could detect that.*

H

P.S. YOU ARE A STUNNING GIRL

* * *

I WAS ALSO writing more frequently for the *Daily Mail.* Sometimes I pitched the ideas to Harold who, if he liked a suggestion, told me to send it to Mac Keene on *Femail*; at other times, he suggested topics and themes, of which some took off and others didn't.

Dear, dear Alix,

"It's No Laughing Matter" [an article I suggested about 'laughter lines' or 'crow's feet around the eyes'] *depends enormously on the picture. I see it seven columns wide. It must be just right; and is deceptively difficult to get just right. It isn't a picture you'll simply "find" some place. Would Dennis* [my American photographer flatmate] *like to have a shot at this? Not if it's something which doesn't interest him tho'; if it's not his line.*

Here is the last edition of "Life". Some superb stuff in it. Its death saddens me. Please don't lose it.

P.S. Don't be disturbed about the German mags and insomnia. [I had suggested a feature on sleeplessness to Femail, then found an in-depth piece in a German glossy.] *Momentarily disappointing for you, but there are good reasons, I assure you, for postponement.*

In the end, my flatmate Dennis did take the photos of women's eyes, crinkled with laughter, for my article – but Harold reported that he had asked for an exceptionally high fee and was therefore unlikely to get more work on the *Daily Mail.*

Hi – and Hello!

I'm very pleased (for what that matters!) with the stuff this morning; nice touch at the last paragraph of the crow's feet piece and the item on the other page was useful, more than useful.

Come to think of it (and I must say this with caution, I must think of it) the eyes article could lead off something like...

YOU AND YOUR LOOKS IN '73

Could be a useful element in these pages (so much more effective now we're back getting two of them fairly often). What would the next one be? The off-obvious headline is important. Say five in all...

I got your note on my desk (clearly a rebuke for losing things!) and Mac has been given them. The advertising piece I see personally (but could be argued out of it) for the International Page; the other as a full feature job. "Sleep", I mean.

What are they paying you? I hope reasonably (but you would be foolish to be unreasonable and ask for payment beyond your range of experience). There's a long way to go (she is 55 after all!) before you can work with the polish and authority of Anne Scott-James (one of the best), see cutting, a beautifully done job.

You see, this is the problem with Dennis (not that I expect he minds). I ask him just to do an experimental shot on something any one of half a dozen photographers on the staff would have done as well. And he argues me up to a silly figure – silly for just the first try-out. It simply means I shan't trouble him again, whereas we might have used him quite often again conceivably.

However, all this is between you, me and these four walls or the gate-post or whatever it is.

I did try to ring you last evening (I didn't get back until nearly 3 o'clock) but you were out. I rang about the cock-up on the seats again.

It's the doghouse for me!

But I have got the record of "Cowardy Custard" [the recording of a theatrical revue featuring the songs of Noel Coward] *which you may like.*

Take encouragement from today's paper. With the town so short of ideas – it's the original idea which is the starting point – I see no reason why (not to exaggerate) you shouldn't make yourself £60 a week by selective outside writing. One has to persevere. Get to know the right people. Work on them.

Harold

* * *

Inevitably, some of my suggested articles fell by the wayside. Some did not interest Harold, as I learned from his muted response: they were either too vague and whimsical, insufficiently fleshed out, or lacked the all-important spark of originality. There were some he did like and told me to pass on to *Femail*, only for them to be rejected by the editor, Mac Keene. I took any such rejections in my stride: a career in theatre and TV had taught me to take rejection philosophically and with good humour. Acutely aware of my inexperience, I was still amazed and counted myself lucky every time I did land a commission.

Occasionally, Harold might come up with suggestions on a topical theme, some of which also failed to take off. I regarded this spontaneous bouncing around of ideas as an essential exercise to free and flex the mind, in much the same way that dance classes or singing practice limber up the body and tune the vocal chords. Only this was more fun. Especially when, in a devilish mood, he would magic up some droll or whacky idea and run with it.

Darling Alix,

Brief bulletin... in lieu of meeting, which is sad.

ITEM. You ought to think up two or three more to go with THE LORD LONGFORD MACINTOSH . My editor [David English] *may not agree, of course, but the paper needs what I could turn this idea into if I could get the right artist (even our own Emmwood would do this with a lot of bite).* [Emmwood was the cartoonist John Musgrave Wood, the Yorkshire-born artist from a family of painters, whom Harold first worked with on the Daily Express and who went on to be the Daily Mail's chief cartoonist for eighteen years before resigning in 1975.] *It would add some spirit of fun to the paper which all papers need: all are too solemn.*

FLASH ! EMMWOOD INVADES

FEMAIL FASHION PAGES

No.1 THE LORD LONGFORD MACKINTOSH

Then the drawing mit the words.

Could we then have... THE DIANA DORS BRA

Throw it away and she bruises her knees (she actually said so last week).

Maybe. I'm not sure... But four of the Lord Longford etc. ideas would

bring a smile – I mean running on successive days – to those pages, which they badly need.

ITEM. All that was wrong with those interviews [I sent him several of my on-spec interviews with women in physically demanding jobs like bus conductors, air stewardesses, ballet dancers, about how their job created specific beauty problems] *is that they needed some work on them. But they did need some work, you know, to be perfectly honest.*

Alas, Mac did not see their possibility. The potential is there, but I'd be dishonest to say the technique is not a little rough and they also are too heavy & solemn! A bus conductor's blackheads do call for a little more finesse, my love.

ITEM. Sorry as I am that I didn't get my hands on these pieces – yes, I know the reason & thank you – I'm in much more despair about this next item. I'll devote my life to getting that bloody diary situation fixed. I'll stand there with hands held out. "Chandelier" is even worse. Avril [his secretary at Chandelier] *had assured me everyone had been paid up on that last issue. I rang her in Yorkshire this morning. Two people hadn't: you... and myself. Monday.*

ITEM. I talked to Anthea Disney [features editor of the Daily Mail] *about the real scene re "I and Albert"* [a new musical about Queen Victoria and Prince Albert, directed by John Schlesinger and starring a former boyfriend of mine as Disraeli, which I anticipated, correctly, would be a flop]. *It didn't bear much resemblance to what she wrote. With uncanny reflection of your own views, she reported the two Americans, one is the lyric writer, as saying: "The bloody English simply don't know how to set about an original musical".*

Wise Alix, beautiful Alix. Love, Harold

* * *

While the journalism was making progress, my domestic environment was far from harmonious. I know Harold thought of my home life as a non-stop roller coaster ride. Just as well there was no CCTV recording the comings and goings on our top floor at Portman Mansions! The footage would have revealed a changing cast of oddball characters who might have stepped out of a Ray Cooney farce and all either came to live or temporarily doss down at my flat throughout the 1970s and early 1980s. Apart from various boyfriends, these were either long-term or short-term flatmates, each with his or her friends and visitors.

Over the years, Harold got to know some of the characters that passed through this ever-revolving door, but this didn't diminish his puzzlement at what he regarded as my chaotic home life.

A frequent irritation was the failure of some of my flat sharers to pay the rent on time – if at all. Such as the Byronic "bearded one", as Harold called Dennis, the American photographer, who would charm his way out of settling the monthly rent on time, assuring me a cheque would arrive at the end of the month – which it never did. Finally, when my mother and I gave Dennis a fortnight's notice to move out, his successor, Esam, a Moroccan friend of Bernard Hall's from Paris, proved another dud. Since Esam spoke hardly any English and worked half the night in a café, blundering into the flat noisily at dawn and rising mid-afternoon to prepare a cooked Moroccan breakfast, his tenure was short-lived.

So too was that of Ap, a polite, reserved eighteen-year-old Dutchman on a gap year, the current squeeze of one of my closest gay friends, Tony Crutchley, a stage manager, director and production assistant at London Weekend Television whom I had known since I was seventeen, and was a frequent visitor to Portman Mansions. With a beaky hauteur reminiscent of Dame Edith Sitwell and a honking laugh that he let rip with all the abandon of a foghorn on speed, Tony was a one-off, even in the camp purlieus of show business.

What I loved about him was his quick mind and rapier wit coupled with formidable learning and intelligence, qualities that belied his infinite capacity for kindness, understanding and empathy. He was one of my closest confidantes, the person I trusted most to share every heartache, problem and intimacy, knowing I could count on his understanding and compassion. Although Tony had two sons from an early marriage, he never pretended not to be gay and was entirely at ease with his sexuality.

On first meeting him, however, strangers, especially non-theatricals, were immediately blown away by Tony's colourful storytelling, complete with double entendres, innuendo, swooping diphthongs and extended vowels. His voice and manner was of a style perfected by the several great British comedians – a fact not lost on Harold when he invited me to bring Tony round for a cup of tea.

Darling Alix,

Your friend is fantastic. Of course you're accustomed to him but, coming on him fresh so to speak, the effect is cyclonic: nicely cyclonic - a really tremendous speed of mind.

But the effect is also uncanny (tho' you'd better not tell him this): close your eyes - I did momentarily! - and it's pure Kenneth Williams you're listening to.

H

8

Revolving Doors

SOON AFTER AP moved out of Portman Mansions, he returned to university in the Netherlands, got a first class degree and became a documentary filmmaker; several years later, he married and started a family. David Steele, Ap's successor as my flatmate, was a young English caterer and chef, who provided some refreshing middle-class stability and restraint, often bringing home delicious leftovers from the BAFTA canteen in Piccadilly where he worked. Meanwhile, my flamboyant and beautiful flatmate Nadia Chigerovitch – whom Harold referred to variously as "the Russian noblewoman" (like me, she had a Russian father) and "Lady Librium" because of her requests for tranquillisers when assailed by emotional upheavals – had moved into a flat on the other side of Marylebone Road. Harold was perpetually amused by Nadia's high drama lifestyle and her proximity to the theatre and show business celebrities, like Elaine Stritch. This sometimes resulted in free theatre tickets or invitations to join her at the Old Vic, where she worked as a PA, then the home of the National Theatre under the directorship of Laurence Olivier.

But the more Harold discovered the quirks and foibles of my flatmates – some of whom, like Bernard 'BJ' Hall, Marlene Dietrich's alcoholic and waspish factotum, he got to know quite well – the more concerned he became over the way this unconventional domestic setup was affecting me personally. Although I was long used to the ups and downs of flat-sharing, Harold's reaction to some of my particularly hair-raising tales eventually made me question whether I hadn't underestimated the stress of the situation.

Darling Alix,

Your last paragraph... never!

Never! You never "look dreadful", unquote. It's just that I think exchanging The Bearded One for Ap, and Ap for Esam (on the basis that you need the rent but never get it!) is quite simply mad. And it takes its toll.

The Welsh Mountain [Simon Jenkins, with whom I was going out and, through me, had hired Harold's housekeeper Queenie to clean his bachelor pad] *says he's got his beef on in today's World at One* [Simon loathed the new London Bridge which replaced the old structure]. *I'll believe it when I hear it.*

You couldn't face Stritch again Thursday evening if I'm still on my feet, could you? I have two tickets but I imagine "Small Craft Warnings" can't be faced more than once. I fully understand.

Love Harold

Once he got to know some of my friends and flatmates better, Harold soon recognised their various faults and foibles – which I put up with, but which he saw as potentially damaging.

Like Bernard Hall's alcoholism.

Dearest Alix,

Sorry about your problem. Strange; I had no idea it was that bad. Alcoholics cause havoc. As I am one, I know! Keep me posted, will you? And, remember, it's tough on the "patient" too. How long is it now, fourteen years or so, "since liquor passed my lips" - but, wow! It's a battle while it lasts. Mary's death aside, toughest thing I ever faced: my own pretty serious seven months in hospital, mostly paralysed, car injuries, pale, compared with the alcohol struggle.

Alcohol? I have this birthday bottle for you, remember? Either this weekend, or on June 1, the Queen's "official" birthday?

Love, Alix... and please my best to your Mum.

H

It was strange that Bernard Hall, of all my camp male friends, was the one Harold got to know best. Maybe because Bernard had got hold of Harold's phone number – simply by looking it up in the phone directory. Harold might dismiss being 'ex-directory' as the ultimate affectation, but I knew it was more of a curse than a blessing when trying to keep certain people at bay, such as BJ with his habit of phoning friends to share breaking dramas in the middle of the night. As when I was working in Paris and he phoned me at 4am to declare that Noel Coward, whom he knew, had died.

Darling Alix,

Just had quite a chat with your mother - I called you there as I thought you'd probably gone to the farm as there seemed no activity hereabouts very late.

Bernard Hall rang me in the middle of the night (didn't disturb me, don't worry). He won't be in Paris this weekend. He wanted to apologise for saying "sod off, you bitch" or words to that effect, when you recently telephoned him in a Nembutal stupor or whatever.

He will be over next week. Had you better warm the sheets and chill the champagne?

A strange episode...

But, let me repeat, I'm personally not in the least put out by it. Truly. Glad to be of help.

What does your mother make of Bernard?

Love, H

Alcoholism and poor time-keeping were only two of Bernard's problems: another was his love of conspiracy, indiscretion, and a habit of manufacturing colourful gossip.

Darling Alix,

Sorry I can't offer you lunch but if you are around at 1.30 or 2 pm, could I give you a drink or a cup of coffee so that at least we could catch up?

TAKE IN NO MORE ARABS, MONTPARNASSE ECCENTRICS OR THE CAST OF "SMALL CRAFT WARNINGS"...

"Doucement, doucement," say I again. You were in a terrible state when I bumped into you in our increasingly elegant elevator.

Love

Harold

PS In real haste en route to the lawyers but just got your note. Of course I spoke to Dietrich's manager [Bernard]. *Don't continue this game of trying to "gaslight" me. I made three bloody calls to France – and Hall thinks that in Suffolk lies the solution. I think in Suffolk lies the solution to nothing!*

BUT

NO

KIDDING,

KIDDO.

The reference to Suffolk was Bernard's attempt to second-guess my relationship with Kendrick Owen, a delightful actor friend I had met when both of us were in a TV play. Ken was also a talented artist and had a studio in Suffolk where he would escape for days or weeks at a time to paint. Although well into middle age, he was something of a wild child, avoiding all routine, convention, and commitment. We would meet for coffee, visit museums and art galleries and enjoy one another's company but, although he was great fun, his extreme eccentricity and fondness for dressing like Worzel Gummidge made it difficult for him to fit entirely into even my relatively unconventional circle of friends.

I soon realised that although Harold loved to meet my more oddball friends, at heart he sought stability and a familiar environment in his life, in short the very opposite of the ever-changing, volatile climate next door.

Dearest Alix,

I can only at this point take a preliminary glance at this stuff [an outline of an idea for a magazine series] *but it does look* <u>*very*</u> *interesting to me.*

So are you: very interesting, I mean. Last night I found you in great form; lively and articulate as ever and, outwardly at any rate, running very buoyantly.

Your life – with <u>*all*</u> *those assets you have (or am I just a simple dewy-eyed fan?) – remains a puzzlement to me.*

Is it that within you there's a compulsion to get involved with messed-up men? Always in the background: a) a broken marriage and the <u>*problem*</u> *of the children – oh, the* <u>*problem*</u> *of the children; or b) the semi 'bent' brigade; c) manifest humbugs and charlatans; d) hangers-on of Lady Librium and her like (tho', admittedly, there aren't many like Lady Librium).*

Is it, I repeat, that in the secret places of your heart, you enjoy dicing around with the desperately unlikely? Thou protesteth not but dos't thou fool thyself?

Time will tell - and quickly.

I've got my ear-muff hat (but we'll talk 'ere I go). In the end, it all seems a bit odd spending Christmas in godless Moscow.

Love. And press on.

H

I was touched, even taken aback by his concern for my wellbeing. I also suspected that while I believed I could blithely sail unscathed above the stresses of flat-sharing, Harold had spotted the underlying reality: I was far from impervious to some of my flatmates from hell and their disruptive influences. After Harold's third or fourth letter, I realised I wasn't kidding anyone, least of all him.

Darling Alix,

Though (he says somewhat pompously!) I am very concerned about my own health, I'm not totally unconcerned about you, either.

And I think you, too, should be taking some steps to "watch it".

On the surface you were, agreed, on great form last night but my impression is that you are looking far from well and the various pressures are reflected in this sense of strain, which is very apparent.

Firstly, I think this mild attack of chicken pox (which people seem to have laughed off) has taken it out of you a bit.

But, probably more important, the strains of your eccentric menage (amusing enough as material for the raconteur) may affect you more than you think, because these things can actually cease to be funny and become a drag, a total bloody drag, when someone of your age, talents, personality and (that old thing!)"good looks" ought to be up and away, over the hills and deep into mischief!

I think it's the blanket of uncertainty that's smothering you - one plan one day, another the next, a non-stop switch of direction, which is bloody well not your fault but debilitating and exhausting for all that.

I also think that this is strictly "none of my business" but I don't want a menage to become a men...agerie and you are one of those behind bars. Sorry. But I DON'T

I am shortly on my way to one residence or another.

Watch it... my love!

H

* * *

Far removed from that inner circle of chaos was one flatmate of whom Harold was especially fond. "The delectable Helen" as Harold called her was a nurse at the Middlesex Hospital who, with Nadia, had been a flatmate of mine for several years before she married an American radiologist and moved to Houston, Texas. Blonde, extremely pretty and charming, Helen Biden and her parents became my second family and weren't in the least fazed by my crazy show business connections – despite the family's associations with the Royal Air Force and the Royal Family. This had come about through Helen's twin sisters, both talented horsewomen, who competed with Princess Anne in cross-country and dressage events such as the Burghley Horse Trials, which I was invited to attend. One twin, Pattie, was a riding instructor who kept her horse in stables at Princess Anne and

Mark Phillips' estate at Gatcombe Park, while her sister Carol, also a horsewoman, eventually became Princess Anne's chef.

In spite of their solidly conservative background, Helen and her parents couldn't have been less stuffy. Among their closest friends was the lyricist Tim Rice, whose mother Joan had been in the WAAFS during the war with Dorothy Biden and whose father, like Helen's father, Murphy, served during the war in the Air Force: after 1945, both men went on to work at a senior level in the aviation industry at Lockheed, and later at Hawker Siddeley.

At the time Helen, Nadia and I shared the flat, Tim Rice and Andrew Lloyd Webber had just written *Jesus Christ Superstar* and were on the verge of signing a contract with the producer Robert Stigwood to bring out a 'stand alone' recording of the show, at the time described as an 'oratorio': the album was to be a precursor to a full-scale stage production in New York and London. The release of a so-called 'concept album' was unprecedented and made big news in show business and in the music industry: before *JCS*, no album of a show had ever been marketed commercially prior to the opening of the show itself. While this back-to-front venture was a huge gamble for Stigwood, as well as for Tim and Andrew, it soon paid off and very soon the Broadway production of *JCS* went into rehearsal.

The entire Biden family and their friends were as excited at Tim's success as he was. In between various girlfriends, Tim would visit the flat for supper, mainly to see Helen – and more. Judging by the men's loafers I occasionally glimpsed in the hall during the early hours of the morning, I realised that the two, who had known one another since childhood, were a perfect example of what we today call 'friends with benefits'. Harold, who once or twice passed Tim on our landing, had kept an eye on his career since the early days of *Joseph and the Technicolour Dreamcoat.*

Dear Alix,

A small New Year present for you (on the doorstep: just

propaganda, really – (inept, appallingly crude propaganda) in favour of the basically – unlikely – Very Important Pharaoh Project.

It would be/HAVE BEEN/ a good idea to go/HAVE GONE/ on to Addis Ababa, where they are frantically fitting little red Sanyo portables into mud huts (seriously) – one leap from barbarism to the Electronic Age with no intervening period of civilisation, just like America.

Sunshine – no clouds at all – where the ageing Lion of Judah sits.

H

If – but I hope I don't – if I can't get back, salutations please to Mr Rice. In the tidal wave of success which so deservedly sweeps over him, he's unlikely to remember the ridiculous back-of-the-font follies which involved me in "Joseph" at St Paul's. Tell him also, please, my money is on the Dean of St Paul's to be President of the Corporation in Canterbury itself, before long.

At the time, the Dean of St Paul's, The Very Reverend Martin Sullivan, a New Zealander, was a delightfully unstuffy character, so unconventional it wasn't surprising he caught Harold's eye. A lover of contemporary and pop music, he founded a programme called *Pop into St Paul's*, encouraging young Londoners and tourists to visit the cathedral, if not for prayer, then to enjoy pop music and sing-alongs. Rev Sullivan had an instinct for publicity when it came to getting bums on pews. At the launch of the first pop-in event, the Dean abseiled down the West Front of the cathedral from Wren's dome, to welcome his flock.

In the late 1960s, after Tim Rice and Andrew Lloyd Webber, then still at school, had composed their first 'pop oratorio', *Joseph and the Technicolour Dreamcoat*, its third performance, after a try-out at Central Hall Westminster, was at St Paul's – when Harold had last met and conferred with Tim Rice behind the font.

The Dean was one of the pair's biggest fans, and wrote a foreword to the original pre-show album of *JCS*. Although he planned to put on the work in the cathedral, and, according to rumour, came up with the brilliant wheeze of inviting John Lennon to star as Jesus Christ, by that time there was too much commercial hype and serious financial interest in *JCS* for the project to take off. Sadly, the Very Reverend Martin Sullivan was never up for the 'top job' at Canterbury, as Harold anticipated. Instead, he returned to New Zealand, where he became a successful author but died unexpectedly in 1980 aged seventy.

When Nadia moved out of the flat, another old friend, Robin Lang, whom I first met in Scotland with Tony Crutchley, joined Helen and me as a flatmate. Several years younger than us, he was then a post-graduate political science student at the London School of Economics where his tutors included two giants of left-wing political science, Ralph Miliband and Ralf Dahrendorf. Robin was affectionately dubbed "your Maoist friend" by Harold, who commissioned him to write a couple of articles for *Chandelier* which I felt were above my head, or beyond my ken.

Robin had counted himself a staunch Marxist-Leninist since his school days in Perth – where Tony Crutchley, a diehard Tory, claimed the brightest pupils, like Robin, had been brainwashed by extremists from the International Socialist movement. Chubby-faced, prematurely balding and whip-smart intellectually, with highly evolved political views, Robin's gentle nature, almost childlike sense of fun and his infinite kindness and warmth won him many close friends, including me. Despite impressive academic qualifications, fluency in French and writing talents, he was in no hurry to find a 'proper' job and chose instead to drift through casual employment until he founded his own French-English London-based film dubbing company.

These jobs included working on an oil rig in the North Sea off Aberdeen, doing film reviews and bits of journalism – including several articles for Harold – and working the lights at a number of Soho's popular strip clubs. These Soho gigs came up through Tony Crutchley, whose friend Kim Kinney, a former actor, staged most of the strip shows, often assisted by Tony moonlighting from his regular job as stage manager at London Weekend Television.

Tony's Soho connection led to two even odder hirings. Robin's Scottish girlfriend Sheilagh, a trained opera singer, came down to London to be with Robin and, while looking for singing work, was persuaded to become a stripper in some of Kim and Tony's shows. Since most of the clubs were owned and run by the same owner, Don Ward, and ran two daily non-stop shows between the hours of midday and 6pm, followed by a second six-hour shift between 7pm and midnight, Sheilagh and many of the other girls could earn good money by dashing between the clubs, all less than five minutes away from one another, to perform in the day and the evening shows.

Eventually, Sheilagh flourished in her new metier to the point where she left Robin and moved to Japan with a new boyfriend, to carry on stripping for far higher wages. Robin too had signed on for double shifts at the same clubs and was eventually joined by John Morton, an Anglo-American friend and fellow postgraduate student from LSE, who shared Robin's love for Pink Floyd and The Grateful Dead, the counterculture and left wing politics. John was hired to operate the lights at the same Soho strip clubs, and was soon promoted to stage manager, eventually moving to the old Essoldo Cinema in Chelsea's Kings Road, where he and his wife Jean, a freelance journalist for the US press, worked in the same capacity on the smash hit, *Rocky Horror Show*.

John, a handsome man whose daily garb included African sandals, chambray shirt and jeans, a batik bandana neckerchief and blond hair pulled back in a long pony tail, had an even more diverse and chequered career than Robin. His distinguished family background was in the US Navy and although he read political science at university, he managed to drift into acting and worked in fringe theatre, TV and films, including John Schlesinger's *Yanks*, *A Bridge Too Far*, *Flash Gordon*, *Superman II* and BBC TV's

Oppenheimer. Eventually, he gained a cult following as Dak Ralter in the early *Star Wars* film, *The Empire Strikes Back*, a following which continues to this day. Finally, he turned his back on show business and returned to the US to write books for the US Navy and act as a communications director for the Pentagon, at the Department of Homeland Security.

I soon discovered Robin and John were keen users of LSD and cannabis, although their drug use was generally moderate, well controlled and produced no noticeably unpleasant behaviour, merely the occasional giggly, good-natured ramblings over a late night cup of tea, followed by a lie-in. Despite Robin's frequent offers to roll me a spliff, I remained impervious to the alleged delights of turning on and dropping out. With good reason.

Several years earlier, while still working in the theatre, I was going out with Roger Schlesinger who took me to a party given by his film director brother, John. On the way there, we picked up the actress Julie Christie, who had baked a stash of 'Hash Brownies' to take to the party. Also known as 'Alice B. Toklas Cake', these delicious chocolate concoctions were laced with strong Moroccan hashish. After midnight, towards the end of the party, where wine, champagne and spirits had flowed lavishly, we tucked into Julie's brownies with gusto.

By the time Roger drove me – and his sixteen-year-old nephew Ian Buruma who was staying with him – home, I started having a panic attack complete with a galloping heart rate, restricted breathing and a rising tide of nausea. Back home, I was violently sick. The next morning, I discovered that Ian had also started throwing up at Roger's flat, leaving his uncle to minister to him throughout the night before leaving for work after a sleepless night.

Since that evening, I steered clear of all mind-altering drugs. I always abhorred the prospect of losing self-control and being stoned represented a horror every bit as distressing and disabling as being drunk and hung over – something I learned to avoid as a teenager after foolishly trying to look grown-up by drinking too much at show business parties.

As flatmates, Robin and Helen made a perfect duo, with Helen's calmness, practicality and down-to-earth nature a perfect contrast to Robin's laid-back, good-natured ramblings about the inequities of capitalism and his support for the almost continuous industrial action and wildcat strikes blighting life in Seventies Britain.

When Helen announced that she and her boyfriend, an American radiologist she'd met at The Middlesex Hospital, were planning to marry and move back to his home town of Houston, Texas, I was ecstatic for her, though she had become a very special friend and I would miss her greatly. Harold was delighted to hear about her engagement and invited her, and me, for a celebratory lunch at the Caprice: "to give her a great send-off".

Dearest little friend,

Two tickets herewith. My God, I hadn't realised it was this hour! The theatre gets earlier and earlier.

If the delectable Helen is in the vicinity, please give her my warmest wishes. I'm a winter wedding man myself – but remember: marriage may be ephemeral – divorce is sacred!

I talked to your mum yesterday by way of clearing up Thursday's misunderstanding. It would have been a wonderful day for the country.

I had a very funny letter from the aggressive David Lewin about the imposing Nadia However-you-spell-her-name.....

Love

Harold

When Dorothy Biden sent out invitations for Helen and her fiancée Howard's engagement party at the Savoy Hotel, Harold was, of course, on the guest list along with Nadia, me, and a couple of other erstwhile denizens of Portman Mansions. The plan was that he would be my escort.

Darling Alix,

Terribly sorry about "Operation Distraught". My trouble – foolishly probably – is that when anxieties and problems are heavy I tend to "hunker down" (in the American phrase) rather than open up. And I really had a sickening experience yesterday.

I wrote a couple of days ago what I hope was a civilised note to Mrs Biden, saying how sorry I was that I couldn't make it. And, I regret this, Alix, but for a variety of reasons too long to go into, it's better to say "no" now than "yes" and then find myself laid up. (The doctor absolutely forbids Paris – more of that later). It would have been nice to have accompanied <u>*you*</u> *(I don't have to stress this !) but you're better off with one of "the crowd" there.*

Likewise my warmest thanx about the suggestion re supper afterwards, but I guess one regretful "no" goes with another. Please pass on my apologies and disappointment to Nadia.

You have the tickets for "Private Lives" anyway; and we'll try to sort arrangements out for that lunchtime today if you're in.

I still owe you last month's "Chandelier" cheque. I'll fix to include payment for the Advertising piece with that. The rest (Apart from "You and your Looks in '73") you'd better fix up with Mac [Mac Keene the editor of Femail]. *I dare say he could get the cheque for the ones published (along with Dennis's) advanced before payment day if this is necessary.*

How do you stand on Paris & New York? Are things <u>*moving*</u>*? I hope in a better direction than mine....*

Love Harold

I was often worried when I didn't hear from Harold for long periods, especially once it emerged his silence was due to ill health.

When the going got rough, he tended to disappear suddenly, either into hospital or confined to his bed, sometimes with twenty-four-hour home nursing. On such occasions, dispatches from his sick bed were infrequent.

Dearest Alix,

Don't imagine I'm feeling too pleased with myself about this total non-communication.

But this time it was no half-measure matter. When I go out of circulation I go out of circulation. Exclamation point!

I have not had one single visitor (with the exception of Sarah's [his secretary] *kind call each evening mit stuff of various kinds); NOT ONE VISITOR AT ALL.*

And believe it or not, no telephone calls – not even to such colleagues as D. English Esq.

Two days ago there seemed some likelihood of a slight further complication – but this seems to be at bay, as of now. I hope.

My 24-hour nursing coverage is a mixed-personality menu – but the day sister is quite something in efficiency (also straight out of a play; also to be filed under the heading "Strict Disciplinarian"). She has on a couple of occasions tried a knock at your door to explain my "withdrawal" – to the point of bad manners, it must have seemed.

I can now make the odd telephone call. And I'll at least today try around 6pm in my interim twixt nurses!

Maybe some time today or tomorrow we may confer briefly. I miss you, Miss Kirsta! All part of my punishment, it may be argued, for a badly organised life.

Meantime the world of evil from the incredible world of Watergate via the noblemen Lambton and Jellicoe, not to mention our former cabinet minister... Sunken Glandys.

And I'm terribly dismayed about Kenneth Allsop.

Love H

The "evil" in this case involved lurid coverage of the sexual exploits of two Tory peers, Lord Lambton and Lord Jellicoe, both ministers in Edward Heath's government. Lord Lambton had just resigned as Minister for the RAF after he was photographed in bed with two prostitutes, smoking cannabis. Within days, the Leader of the House of Lords, Lord Jellicoe, also resigned, after being found to have used prostitutes procured by a woman who ran the same escort agency favoured by Lord Lambton.

Far from being a prude, Harold was dismayed at how these scandals undermined British politics and the credibility of the government. His jokey aside about "Sunken Glandys" referred to another prominent minister, Duncan Sandys, also making headlines after being caught up in out some recent financial skulduggery.

A previous Tory Minister of Defence and Winston Churchill's son-in-law, Sandys had been forced to repay £44,000 to the company Lonrho after he previously accepted a compensation payment of £130,000 from its CEO Tim 'Tiny' Rowlands, for giving up a lucrative consultancy with the firm. It later emerged that Sandys had hidden the sum in a Cayman Islands account to escape paying British tax.

Unfortunately for Sandys, every time his name came up in the popular press, it prompted sniggers over his past sex life. His name first emerged during the notorious 1963 divorce case of Margaret Duchess of Argyll as one of the Duchess's eighty-eight other lovers, when he was alleged to be the 'headless man' featured in Polaroid photos taken of the Duchess performing sex acts with numbers of unidentified men.

All these cases of Tory sleaze were, of course, prime tabloid fodder and may have diverted Harold fleetingly, but in fact disgusted him. By comparison, his dismay at the suicide of the TV broadcaster and current affairs presenter Kenneth Allsop, whom he knew, was deep and genuine. It was a tragic end to a brilliant career. Allsop, an erudite man who suffered from extreme and chronic pain after the loss of a leg following the war, was a respected author and campaigning naturalist who apparently suffered one blow too many to keep marching on.

When he was unceremoniously fired from his position as books editor and chief book reviewer on the *Evening News* for "using words over the average reader's head", he approached the editor of the *Evening Standard*, Charles Wintour – father of *Vogue* editor Anna Wintour –asking if he could contribute book reviews to the newspaper. However Wintour refused, saying no opportunities were available. Allsop, no stranger to depression for much of his life, and having a tendency to drink too much, took the rejection badly, returned to his home in Dorset and took an overdose of barbiturates.

Tragedies such as these always affected Harold deeply and reminded me of his big, compassionate heart. With his own experience of chronic illness and the ravages of alcohol, he empathised strongly with a troubled man like Kenneth Allsop. Crucially, he also had been around Fleet Street long enough to recognise the harshness, cruelty and indifference within the industry that could push even hardened journalists to the edge.

9

The Department of High Drama

If my life was a roller coaster, then Harold's, as he was the first to acknowledge, was no less chaotic. I first suspected as much when his flat and mine were both burgled on the same night. Thieves had broken into my flat through a skylight and stolen a vast number of clothes, jewellery and antique objects belonging to my parents, leaving every cupboard and drawer ransacked, their contents disgorged, like an avalanche over the floor. The next day I ran into Harold, who told me he too was burgled. It was long before we became friends and all I could do was commiserate and when he said the thieves had made off with a large amount of silverware and other valuables, I brightly pointed out that at least our respective house insurance policies would cover the losses.

He shook his head with a balefully expression. "I'm not insured. The policy recently ran out and I forgot to renew it." Since my mother had always drummed into me that adequate insurance against burglary and domestic accidents was a prerequisite to living in London, I was genuinely aghast. Since

Harold was by then divorced from his second wife, the flighty Susan, and only had a secretary at work to deal with his business affairs, I realised his home life must be a bit of a mess.

Several years later, after we had become friends, he and I were burgled again. This time our front doors had been forced open when no one was at home. Again, the thieves trashed our apartments and took a lot of valuables. On this occasion, Harold confided that the burglars accidentally brought something important to his attention, something he had long forgotten. Many years earlier, he was given a revolver for which he had no licence. The revolver remained hidden at the back of one of his bedroom cupboards, underneath piles of clothes, and when the burglars rifled through his wardrobe they inadvertently threw or kicked the gun into the middle of the room. Realising that when he reported the burglary, police would check the crime scene for fingerprints and other forensic evidence, he panicked. Possession of a firearm without a licence is a criminal offence.

"What did you do?"

"When I came home last night and discovered the burglary, I noticed the gun on the floor. I realised I had to get rid of it at once before calling the police."

"How?"

"I got into the car, drove to Regent's Park and threw the gun in the lake from the bridge on the Inner Circle just by the entrance to the tennis courts."

I knew instantly why he had chosen that spot. In the 1960s, he often worked from home and would ask his secretary at the *Daily Express* to bring him his mail; after he read it and dictated his replies, she returned to Fleet Street. Usually this exchange took place in Portman Mansions, but in warm, sunny weather he liked to be outdoors and their rendezvous took place at a bench by the Regent's Park tennis courts, where they took care of the correspondence. The bridge and the lake, a stone's throw from the tennis courts, were indelibly imprinted on his memory, even at a time of crisis.

Despite this, it seemed such a bizarre reaction, given that he could probably have acquired a licence for the gun without getting into trouble with the police. But this reaction was pure Inspector Clouseau, a classic bit of business right out of the *Pink Panther*, and it magnificently confirmed his capacity for high drama.

Harold's habit of hiding things and then forgetting where he put them not only got him into trouble, but was also a source of both hilarity and exasperation among his colleagues. He had a long-standing reputation for buying up exclusive and costly photographs when he was on the *Daily Express, Daily Mirror* and *Daily Mail*, to ensure that his own newspaper had a 'scoop' and, more specifically, that the best photos were simply unavailable to rival publications.

His habit of stuffing these pictures, sometimes with other paperwork, under his carpet "for safety" was the stuff of Fleet Street legend. Stories of cleaning ladies retrieving such long hidden treasures while hoovering and attempting to flatten the bumps in his office carpet, even after he left one newspaper office to join another publication, still make the rounds.

Sometimes more than exclusive photographs went missing. On one occasion, Harold was booked to go on a Far East business trip and had taken two thousand pounds, a large sum in the 1970s, from his bank account in advance of the trip. On the day of his departure, he looked in vain for the money at home and at work. As he was about to take a taxi from the *Daily Mail* office to Heathrow, in mounting despair, a senior editor noticed his distress and suggested he might have put the money somewhere safe. Harold duly ran his hand along the edges of his large office carpet until he felt the giveaway bump of an envelope crammed with £50 notes.

Forgetting to renew his insurance, ignoring the renewal of the lease on his flat, late payment of bills and taxes, came partly from his overstretched work schedule as well as a hectic private life. The better I got to know him, the more I realised he found it hard to say no to an invitation, or to cancel a meeting – despite the likelihood that he would have to bow out as the engagement approached.

Dear Alix,

Two in the front row of the circle (I'm assured); that is, if you don't regard anything other than a seat on the aisle, Row F, as socially humiliating? (I do, rather.)

My problem is:

Morning 11.30 – small (six) cocktail party at the "Mail" here for Gene Hackman.

Lunch: Evening Standard Awards (average two and a half hours for the course).

Evening: "Company" first night.

Am I in the newspaper business, or not? When do I get any work done?

Love

HAROLD

Often, when things went awry, it was due to forces beyond his control. Missed theatre performances, lost tickets and mistaken dates could be a consequence of other people's slip-ups.

Dearest Alix,

There has been a cock-up – entirely the fault of my 'temp' secretary. And I can hardly face you.

The tickets she got are for the Joseph Losey production of "The Doll's House" next Friday.

This I learn 20 minutes ago!

Because I forgot to check with her yesterday when I intended to pick them up. My stupidity, this.

Such, however, is my alarm at facing your wrath that

within the last five minutes I've taken a chance and got two for the Criterion tomorrow matinee. I shall go – and I hope you can.

I've got to dash now but I'll ring you as soon as I can.

Maybe we can have dinner tonight.

I grovel in abasement, Harold

After the first such couple of cancellations, I recognised that if two or three such "cock-ups" occurred in succession, it was likely that Harold was under undue stress for various reasons. Significantly, the major stress at such times was likely to be ill health as well as an over-extended schedule.

Dearest Alix,

I do appreciate your patience (who said you hadn't any!) in this puzzlingly tiresome time I'm going through. I imagine it will pass. I imagine so.

On top of everything, I had a most ghastly distressing experience with the Daubenys the day you looked in the office. It dismayed me immeasurably. Ah, the penalty of newspapers.

I'm behaving possibly a little foolishly in health matters, I know (but that's for your ears only). If all is well though, I'm "taking a pull" from today.

Standing at a reception for a couple of hours though, (much as I'd have enjoyed it) was really out – indeed anything except the absolute minimum.

What I am glad about is that you've alternative arrangements for tonight. I loathe and hate letting you down. Put the tickets through the box, will you & I'll pass them on elsewhere. There seems not much difficulty in getting into that theatre now. I'd still like to go if you would. So maybe...

I want to get one or two things (out of about a thousand!) in order in case this time I'm really out of action. I'll be taking, all being well, a rest in bed over lunchtime. If you're around & in the vicinity & care to, give me a call.

Thanx, Alix

Harold

Several days later, a note arrived in a similar vein; his health was clearly still below par and I knew he was making the effort to follow doctor's orders. Diagnosed many years earlier with arrhythmia, a serious heart dysfunction aggravated by years of alcoholism, the condition needed continuous monitoring and periodically flared up, leading to hospital admissions or home nursing. As the years passed, he lived increasingly under doctor's orders and 'Buky', as he called his doctor, seemed to be the only person capable of controlling Harold's workaholism and tendency to burn the candle at both ends. Whatever Buky said, went.

Darling Alix,

There is a book outside the door – I hope that the Keeble magazine/book service occasionally works at speed.

I'm disappointed about tonight. Despite the misunderstanding, I'm most grateful to Nadia for asking me along [my ex-flatmate Nadia had invited us to a play at the Old Vic] *and I'd be grateful if you'd tell her so.*

I'll ring you later about "The Doll's House" tickets. Have them if you wish – I mean this –but I'd quite like to have seen the thing with <u>you</u> another time. But they're yours just by saying so.

Love Harold

Like a top juggler or magician, sleight of hand and decades of practice enabled him to pivot on a sixpence. He swiftly manoeuvred schedules, shifted existing plans or cancelled meetings at the eleventh hour, always with genuine regret and irresistible charm. You couldn't be angry with Harold for long if he bowed out of a social engagement at the last minute. Even his colleagues and the editor of the *Daily Mail* must have been quick to forgive, especially if he went AWOL.

Darling Alix,

I'm not Mr Popular, alas, at Northcliffe House because while I was enjoying Covent Garden, [we had both been at the ballet] *for the first time in the history of the world, the Vice-President of the United States was deciding to resign or else go to prison! It's unbelievable!* [Vice-President Spiro Agnew had resigned after allegations of corruption while he was Governor of Tennessee.] *My sin being that I had left no telephone number where I could be reached. However...*

This page isn't going to please you [a mock-up of an article I had written, about to go to press]. *Incidentally, I've restored some stuff cut out.*

But, but...

The facts in the paragraph ringed are undeniable, it seems. [A date I had reproduced was incorrect.]

And what you might find more intriguing is that this morning we had a "private word" with the power-that-be at Covent Garden, who endorsed that it would be "bang on" to say this about dear Miss Sibley [the Royal Ballet ballerina Antoinette Sibley]. *Apparently "Manon" is going to clinch it for her, so to speak.*

I'll drop in that advance copy of "Cosmo" - but we haven't finished with it yet.

Take your syringe to Paris - and good luck there, too; you may need it.

Love, Harold

It became obvious his real nemesis was bureaucracy. The failure to keep his affairs 'in order' arose through an innate dislike of officialdom, a tendency to turn a blind eye to the rules and regulations making up the small print of everyday life. That partly explained his ambivalence towards the demands made of a newspaper editor. Although he was the editor of the *Sunday Express* for several years in the 1950s, as well as associate and deputy editor of that and the *Daily Express*, his mercurial nature thrived on creative freedom and he was happiest designing, laying out and honing a newspaper's appearance: he was known to redesign a front page sometimes as late as an hour before an edition was due to go to press. Business matters bored him, and he was the first to recognise it – and accept the inevitable consequences.

Dearest Alix,

Feeling faintly foolish about this "poor man's Howard Hughes" taunt of yours - very poor man's, etc!

Didn't get in last night until 10.30 and, having got myself a bite of food, was going to call you but found an old Judy Garland film listed. Not for me; but I imagined you might be hooked on it and understandably I know how you dislike being pulled from the box and it always frightens me a little.

Apart from that, yesterday really started the New Year in great style.

1. Something went amiss with my minor dental operation & I had to have a wildly inconvenient mid-afternoon session in Harley Street.

2. Much worse. Spent lunchtime with my accountant to learn - the bloody flaming idiot! - that the Inland Revenue were calling not for hundreds, but thousands of pounds: truly.

"But I thought you knew, Mr Keeble..." Except there was no letter establishing he'd ever told me!

3. A libel action arising out of the Dietrich piece.

4. The enclosed jolly (and sinister) threat about the rent. Did you get one too? Ouch! I must acknowledge it! [He received a letter informing him that his lease had expired nine months earlier and Hampton & Sons, the managing agents, were sending an assessor to inspect the flat and propose a fair rent before his lease could be extended.]

5. Lost key-ring, really lost it, with all keys on it.

Oh, sundry other things...

Let us repair this overlong non-communication (and I've just remembered I owe you for some tickets).

Please tell Dennis I'll look at these contacts under illuminated magnification probably today and pick one out.

Love

Harold

Much as I sympathised with him over his run-ins with various authorities, his retelling of these episodes was of course vastly amusing – and a part of him must have thought so too.

ALIX the K

ITEM

What lovely weather and how long it continues!

ITEM

Pity I threw that gun away! I could have joyously used it (after 7.30am start) at Reigate Police Court, where I was fined £100 (£220 cost additionally) BECAUSE THE SWANSEA COMPUTER SAYS I DON'T EXIST AND HAVE NEVER HAD A DRIVING LICENCE IN MY LIFE

This is true!

Question: Shall I make history – and be the first man ever to sue a computer?

Keeble versus Computer Charlie X170B

It was ironic that someone as fixated as Harold on high tech and on buying the latest, cutting edge televisions, radios, cameras, videos and cassette recorders, could so easily be defeated by the glitches of intercom systems, erratic transport services and ordinary telecommunications. Although he had a point about the vagaries of British Telecom. At that time, making a phone call on the UK's antiquated wiring system often resulted in crossed lines, wrong numbers and an alarming incidence of crackles, clicks and wheezes once you were fortunate enough to reach the correct number,

Dearest Alix,

I'm sorry you're feeling "downish" – that makes two of us – "caught up in the gale of the world".

I surely am. One nightmare chasing another and nothing (do I dream this?) seems to work. At the station, quite casually they say "The train isn't running," "British Rail regret to announce..." And regret and REGRET and go on regretting. You dial the number you want (tonight yours from a King's X call-box); you dial it with almost imbecilic concentration! First time I got Romford, second, Salisbury, third, 0917 [my number was 0918]. *TRUE! At that point you begin to wonder: am I suffering from some unsuspected brain damage? Maybe!*

I was sorry about tonight. TRULY. No Queenie [his housekeeper]; *no secretary; given the wrong number by Directory of Enquiries for Maison Bertaux* [a Soho patisserie where I told him he would find me having tea if had to cancel our dinner date]. *More "brain damage"!*

It's 2.am and I just have your generous note. Maybe a few hours' sleep (last night three!) and then these early telephone calls (maybe TEN actual diallings) to explain they've decided Heathrow won't bother to function at all today, so please cancel your visit! Did you know the working population ("working"? Je me demande!) at London Airport is 52,000 people in and out every day.

I don't require the magazines etc. outside returned.

And let's try again. ***Let's!***

Love H

* * *

Compared to unpaid taxes, lapsed leases and out-of-date insurance policies, there came a time when the bane of Harold's life – and mine to a lesser extent – was the ancient, rickety lift in our block, which made daily comings and goings a challenge as well as, literally, a step into the unknown. This was the same wretched contraption in which, as a schoolgirl, I had first met Harold stuck midway between floors. In the 1970s, it began increasingly to break down, leaving us to climb five flights of stairs to our flats – something which bothered Harold more and more as his health declined.

The lift was installed in the late 19th century when Portman Mansions was built and by the 1970s was showing every sign of decrepitude. Slow and creaky, it could barely hold two people – three was a crush – while entering and exiting required not only split-second timing, but muscles of steel. Only an engineer from the pre-automation age could have installed a thick wooden external door – aptly called a slab door – on a spring so heavily weighted it had to be hauled or kicked open and held in position to prevent it slamming into one's back or chest. Behind this was another potential killer; an equally weighty, collapsible iron scissor-gate, heavily sprung with a vicious spring-back closing mechanism that, unless you held it open, smashed into your ribs, pinning you against the door frame.

Long-term residents like Harold and me were adept at manoeuvring, kicking and punching our way unscathed out of this vintage death trap. But when the lift began to go out of action for many hours, days, eventually even weeks, Harold went on the warpath.

Dearest Alix,

ITEM. The lift situation has now come to a crisis point, and, with the flat below and Flat H and one other, I seek your support.

I have got the "Mail" lawyers involved. Last night I was stuck between floors for over an hour and only the merest luck saved me from spending the whole night there. Do you realise, the alarm bell unbelievably isn't even wired in to the porter's hide-out?

DO NOT USE THE LIFT. A talkative engineer has talked too much! The actual chances of a sudden death-drop are not formidable, agreed. But they exist.

Would you choose an unserviced pre-war Dakota plane for your next flight? And pay extra for it?

I really am finally incensed about this situation, which is one of plain fraud. Blood – even if it's mine – is going to be spilled. Your mum is the tenant, officially, yes? Please tell her.

ITEM. I caught only the final minutes of your mid-week programme. Repeat Saturday? A quelle heure ? [I had been doing a series of TV dance reviews on BBC TV.]

NOW ABOUT THIS ELEVATOR... ACHTUNG! ACTION!

My mother and I both complained to the managing agents about the condition of the lift. Several neighbours downstairs followed suit. To our surprise, Hampton's acknowledged our complaints and soon announced a refurbishment programme of the common parts; new paintwork, new carpets and a thorough inspection and servicing of the ailing lift. The refurbishment was no doubt well meant, but it only heaped more misery on the tenants.

In the end, it was Harold's letter of complaint to Hamptons that produced results. Masterfully authoritative, it carried a sting as well as the implied threat that revelations about the company's mismanagement of Portman Mansions would, unless rectified, be splashed all over the national press.

From the day he showed me the letter, I made a mental note of the phrase: *incompetence of which good newspaper stories are made.* Words I used frequently over the years when writing letters of complaint to various institutions and their representatives.

It helped that his letter was written on *Daily Mail* headed notepaper.

Dear Sir,

I live in one of your properties: at number 1M Portman Mansions. My files show that I wrote to you not long ago expressing pleasure that a company of your status had taken the property under your control. My letter was appallingly premature, it seems.

I am quite aware that you have had other protests; quite aware that this letter is en route to the wastepaper basket (or shredder); but nonetheless I would like the right people to know that the antics of your organisation in the block where I live (I have the whole top floor) in recent weeks add up to a picture of contemptuous incompetence of which good newspaper stories are made.

In a single sentence, it is the story of how the re-decoration of a staircase, the patching up – no more than patching up – of an unbelievably archaic lift and some rewiring has now inconvenienced all the tenants for three months and is still nowhere near finished.

Alas, this is only the essence of it. One's complaint is the massive disregard of elementary concern for the people who have to live through this incompetence.

Example: without the slightest forewarning of any kind at all, I learned ten days ago (fifteen minutes before they took it out of action) that "you won't have any lift available for a week at least - and maybe a lot longer". This was precisely what the man in charge said.

Now - this you can hardly be blamed for! It so happens that I am convalescing from fairly serious heart trouble; I had been in bed during most of the repainting, rewiring and so on.

There is no question of my being able to walk up five flights of stairs. I have a flat in Brighton where I live at the weekend but had promised it to a friend some while ago and didn't want to disappoint them for their holiday.

Accordingly, I have had to move into a hotel and now another week has gone by and, at lunchtime today, I was told: "We may finish it this week, we may not." Just that.

Had anyone had the courtesy to tell the tenants the lift was being pulled out of action not for hours, but for days, indeed weeks, I could have made other arrangements and saved myself about £300.

Please understand that, presumably, there are good intentions behind this chaos. The fact that the overall result is to give the place a kind of down-graded Golder's Green ambience (one shudders to think what the stairs carpet will be like) is merely a measure of your décor consultant's taste. There it is, poor fellow; and nothing can be done about it.

But I do find it astonishing that a company of your status can behave with total contempt towards its tenants.

As I say, this letter, I fully appreciate, is a total waste of my time. "The dogs bark but the caravan moves slowly - very slowly on", etc.

Nevertheless I would value – officially and for the record – some explanation of what lies behind this truly newsworthy example of incompetence.

Yours,

Harold Keeble.

P.S. I hope you have no objection to my sending a Xerox of this note (written in my hotel) to one other person at Hamptons.

Within twenty-four hours, the lift was back in service. But not for long. The battle resumed; more blood was spilled.

Darling Alix,

I hope I haven't upset Mr Lynch [the head porter], *rather a dear old boy really; and obviously harassed by the newer tenants* [several flats had recently been rented by Middle Eastern families with large numbers of children prone to running amok in the corridors]. *But we are entitled to being pissed off too! Repaired four days after a month's breakage and OUT again. Outrageous!*

I had a terrible row with the so-called administrator of the block, absurdly called Mr Luck! "Do you realise you're speaking to a magistrate?" he said to me.

"I realise I'm speaking to a bloody ineffectual useless fool who should probably never come out of his cellar," I said.

It won't do any good, of course. You and I, kiddo, have got to move.

But poor Lynch – what with waiting for an operation for piles (unpleasant, they tell me) AND the Middle East dregs... Well, I thought he showed great spirit. But why did he go on about PIGS? Do you recall it? PIGS?

Apologies for this memo on a TV Storybook pad – the only paper I have immediately to hand.

Don't see "State of Revolution, Star Wars" when it arrives

E N D

It was around the time of the refurbishment of Portman Mansions and the lift going out of service that numbers of long-standing tenants on the floors below us moved out – often citing unreasonable rent increases: few tenants in those days owned their flats. The old-timers were replaced by numbers of newly wealthy Middle Eastern families from the oil-rich Gulf States, who had begun visiting England either for extended holidays, work commitments or medical treatment in nearby Harley Street and the Wellington Hospital. The families would spend a large part of the year at their London homes, going on massive shopping binges at Harrods, Selfridges and our local Marks and Spencer flagship store in Oxford Street. Come winter, they either returned to the Middle East or commuted between the two counties throughout the year.

Whereas no previous Portman Mansions tenants throughout the decades seemed to have had small children, this now was changing; as far as Harold was concerned, not for the better.

Darling Alix, 3.15 am Sunday

I truly am horrified to learn that we are the last two (one male, one female) Caucasians manning the barricades.

Of course it is ghastly.

I was around Saturday night when the ritual weekend smashing of the lift took place (How can one hope otherwise? I gather that one flat now houses eleven children). Nonetheless, I have had six journeys to the top to make today. One might say: "Why do it?" Not easy sometimes to avoid, if this is where your home is supposed to be.

As often when something odd occurred in Harold's life, or something was afoot and he took me into his confidence, he would turn the incident into a running gag, riffing on a theme such as the changing environment of Portman Mansions. Shortly after the latest *fracas* over the lift, a card with a large illustration of two rhinos crossing horns popped through my letterbox.

Below, in thick red marker pen and one inch capitals, a word under each rhino:

THEM... US

I am advised in no circumstances to drink the tap water on the top floor. "They" are feeding things into the supply which could do us grievous harm - yours of a different nature, a different kind of damage to mine: both unpleasant.

I tell you, Tootsie, these are formidable adversaries!

May The Force Be With You.

10

Impostor Syndrome

The last thing I expected when dipping a toe into journalism was to be swept far outside my existing theatrical circle. As I branched out and interviewed an expanding cross-section of professionals and 'experts', some went on to become friends and in turn introduced me to their own circle – which proved every bit as unconventional as the field of theatre and entertainment.

Among these new contacts and friends was John Stud, a pioneering obstetrician and gynaecologist intent on promoting the emerging wonders of Hormone Replacement Therapy (HRT) for menopausal women in the UK. There was also a delightful fitness expert with his own beauty salon and gym, who eventually brought over a popular range of French skincare products called Décleor, based on plant oils. One woman with whom I became friends, and who eventually even shared my flat for a short time, was a British Airways stewardess and union representative who commissioned me to interview leading British fashion designers for a piece about their views on BA's new staff uniforms for the trade newspaper she edited.

Journalism opened up untold networking opportunities.

This social side of journalism was entirely new to me, with its press conferences, product launches and public relations events which included sit-down lunches, champagne breakfasts and cocktail parties. The events were held in top London hotels and restaurants, mainly to woo and to thank the press, to which, with a sense of disbelief, I realised I now belonged. Or, as I saw it, some people assumed I belonged.

I started to live a double life. One, as an actress attending auditions, interviews and castings for TV plays, films and commercials; going to rehearsals, filming on location and at TV studios including BBC TV Centre, Elstree and Pinewood for days and weeks on end. My other role was as a journalist covering a variety of subjects for different publications.

While my theatre friends knew about my writing and were enthusiastic about what I was doing, no one in journalism, with the exception of Harold, knew about my show business life. When meeting other journalists and carrying out interviews for articles, I began experiencing the weird sensation of trying to pass myself off as a pro in a world peopled by professional hacks – an unsettling phenomenon that is nowadays labelled 'imposter syndrome'.

An unnerving sense of dishonesty and self-consciousness led to the point, even when some new contacts became friends, that I no longer mentioned my theatre and TV career to anyone outside the arts world. Editors, interviewees and other journalists simply assumed I was a hack by training and had at some time worked my way up on some provincial newspaper before arriving in London. To my relief, they never asked for details.

The journalistic environment, however, was gregarious, friendly and welcoming. Every press occasion culminated in a wave of introductions, hasty scribbled names, the swapping of business cards and phone numbers. As my diary filled up with these 'work related' entries, the boundary between social and journalistic dates, like the distinction in my address book between friends, interviewees, PR reps and business contacts, became blurred.

What astonished me was that, far from being dull, pinstripe-suited businessmen, stuffy doctors and buttoned-up academics, some of these new arrivals in my life were extraordinarily eccentric given their professions. Like the tall, elegantly cadaverous Harley Street GP and former ship's doctor now working as an osteopath, who had a fondness for cowboy boots, wore his immaculately highlighted hair jaw-length and paraded a string of young girlfriends. One day, he made the morning news on BBC Radio Four because of a bizarre incident entirely unrelated to his profession. Police had arrested him at dawn on Hampstead Heath, charging him with unlawful possession of a firearm and taking part in a duel with a rival who tried to seduce his girlfriend.

Another new friend often in the news was Peter Stephan, a cigar-chomping millionaire businessman who had set himself up as a self-styled 'youth doctor' in Harley Street. He specialised in a widely publicised form of rejuvenation therapy, boasted a celebrity clientele and had a penchant for red brocade and gilt interiors, gambling and glamorous wives.

Youth therapy apart, Stephan also made headlines when his business partner, a qualified doctor with a practice in Kent, was arrested in America on suspicion of hiring a hitman to assassinate Stephan. The alleged motive was that he expected to inherit Stephan's wealth by taking over the lucrative Harley Street rejuvenation practice. The GP was tried, found guilty and sentenced to several years' imprisonment.

Less colourful but extraordinarily go-ahead was a beauty therapist who was building her own practice near Harley Street after a divorce. Sally Gilbert-Wilson regularly schmoozed the press with catered soirées and invitations to Paris to assess new trends in the French beauty business, which she planned to introduce to London. Sally was enthusiastic about me accompanying her on these 'working trips' to Paris, because she spoke only English and relied on me to translate for her and conduct interviews in French on her behalf. That aside, we shared a love of French food and wine, making the trips genuinely enjoyable.

Networking was a new concept for me, but I soon got the hang of it. Why had I never realised how spontaneous and gregarious people could be outside the confines of show business? At times, the spin-off, both socially as well as professionally, was of inestimable value. Through my friendship with Annie Redmile, aka 'Red Annie', the labour-leaning British Airways union rep and travel correspondent for BBC Radio, I met Keith Howell, a jazz critic working for the newly launched commercial London radio station, LBC. When he found out about my knowledge of theatre and dance and my hope of becoming a dance critic, he suggested I come into the LBC studios off Fleet Street and give an interview on what was currently happening on London's dance scene. I always loved the idea of doing radio and accepted like a shot.

The interview went well, and I was offered a post as LBC radio's dance correspondent, a job I held for three and a half years, broadcasting regularly on new musical shows, ballet and contemporary dance performances, visiting companies, mime and multi-media productions. On two subsequent trips to New York to visit friends and research articles for *Vogue*, I also managed to report back on the New York City Ballet and American Ballet Theatre.

I loved the LBC job. Doing a similar job on TV turned out less successfully. I was hired to front a series of six BBC TV programmes called *What's On In Dance* – delivered straight to camera, sitting alone at a desk reading my own script off an autocue – but the experience failed to inspire me in the same way as the radio work. Despite being experienced and confident at working in front of a TV camera, to my dismay no one gave me tips on reading an autocue: it took me the first programme to work out a way of looking and sounding natural and relaxed. By comparison, radio encouraged familiarity and casualness, and you didn't have to worry what you looked like.

Although more doors were opening, I was still hesitant about my abilities and lacked sufficient confidence to grab every opportunity that came my way. During a brief period when I was going out with the journalist Simon Jenkins, before he became editor of the *Evening Standard* and later *The Times*, he asked me at a few hours' notice if I could review a dance performance for the next day's edition of the *Evening Standard*, since he heard the paper's dance critic was ill. I turned it down, pretending to be busy, when in fact I was panic-stricken and convinced I wouldn't be able to file my copy over the phone within an hour of the curtain coming down and the paper being put to bed. I knew my limitations and working at top speed was one of them.

Although Harold was delighted that I had landed the LBC job and was beginning to embark on more varied work, he was also my sternest critic – for which, of course, I was eternally grateful.

Dear Alix,

Listen! No one really accepts critical comment, however constructive and particularly when it's well meant!

But you've GOT to slow down your speech rate on the LBC Dance Programme. I imagine you have last week's on tape: if not, I have.

And it's not just a matter of speed - talking far too fast for the listener to absorb it.

At the heart is change of pace & length in sentence construction. Truly, and in admiration, there's some excellent writing in what you say (but more to be read than said).

You simply must break up those well-constructed but complicated multi-clause sentences with... BANG! The sudden four-word sentence.

I'm right about this, I know I am.

Love, H

As always, he was right. I never doubted it. I knew how fortunate I was that a newspaperman of his status was not only the first of my editors, but one determined to instil in me the fundamentals of clear, concise reporting and nipping bad habits in the bud. Such as a tendency to string together plonkingly over-long sentences – subordinate clauses and all – which either muddied the page, or hung heavy in the air.

Becoming a critic brought free theatre tickets, invitations to press nights for every musical show in town, including press seats at Covent Garden, allowing me to see productions for which I would have paid a fortune, or missed. Better still, the seats came in pairs, so I could invite friends who had an interest in dance and music. This, of course, included Harold, who was by now a regular theatre-going companion. To my complete surprise, I discovered he shared my appreciation of both classical music and dance and even went so far as to buy me books on certain artists and choreographers, as well as LPs of ballet and classical music – which he often borrowed to listen to alone at home.

Dear Alix,

I did so much enjoy "old times" again last night. I'm <u>very</u> grateful to you. It was a great occasion for me at Covent Garden - and most intriguing the discussion which followed.

Tiny point. I'm not "on", as they say, this morning. But what we have to talk about for "Grattan Mail" can be done on the telephone quite easily. [He asked me to write articles for another publication he edited, the Grattan Mail, published by the owners of the Grattan Catalogue in Yorkshire.] *I will telephone you without fail while you're sorting Mummy out! I mean in the country.*

Again thanx - and great to see you. H

* * *

There was a particularly interesting season at Covent Garden one summer when the opportunity arose to see the works of John Cranko, a major English choreographer who, some years earlier, defected to Germany, where he became Artistic Director of the Stuttgart Ballet Company. Not only was Cranko a great choreographer – one of his latest acclaimed works was a three-act ballet based on Pushkin's *Eugene Onegin* – but the quality of the company he built up was regarded as one of the finest in the world. Cranko's *Onegin* was, therefore, the hot ticket for the company's Covent Garden season, along with his other major three-act work, *Taming of the Shrew*.

Dearest Alix,

I am afraid the choice for me here is an imperative one!

I would have liked to have seen both and of course, we had talked about "Onegin" but on present plans I will be going away for that proposed week on Friday 20th, so I guess I will have to settle for the Thursday. (I guess I am personally lucky the way the dates have fallen, as I think I told you, I did see "Onegin" not long ago in Munich, magnificently done. I hope the arrangement does not disappoint you too much.

Herewith cheque for the tickets. The Cranko evening should be wonderful.

Agree with you about Diana Rigg's brief husband. [I had met the Israeli artist Menachem Gueffen, recently divorced from Diana Rigg after a fleeting marriage, and while I got on well with him, I also found him a bit heavy going and arrogant.] *I was hearing quite a bit more about him last night.*

Harold

Who hopes to set up a rendezvous for a little refreshment together early next week...

Although Harold liked to joke that, since I was so steeped in the arts, he suspected I viewed him as a philistine, of course I never did. On the contrary. His appreciation of great contemporary playwrights was evident, especially when we went together to see plays such as Tom Stoppard's *Jumpers* and *Travesties*, Noel Coward's *Private Lives,* Peter Schaffer's *Equus* and Tennessee Williams' *Small Craft Warnings:* his responses were always informed and acutely analytical. Sometimes it was like going to the theatre with a drama critic. Occasionally, hearing a compelling line of dialogue – I remember especially the line, "Lies are like boomerangs. They always come back and strike the liar," – he instantly reached into his pocket for pen and paper and scribbled it down.

Although by no means a regular operagoer, on his return from a working trip to Venice to "look at Marco Polo's Will" – apparently there was some dispute as to whether Marco Polo had ever visited China or had simply appropriated the experiences of another Italian explorer who went East – Harold told me how impressed he was with Venetian geniality and culture. After a day's work poring over the will with an interpreter at the National Library, he tried to get a ticket at La Fenice Opera House for that night's performance of *La Traviata.*

"The theatre was full and there were no last minute returns or house seats. But the manager was incredibly helpful and charming. He brought a small gilt chair, placed it at the end of the sixth row of the stalls, on the aisle, and invited me to watch the performance. It was a delightful evening. And the opera was superb."

Far from knowing too little about dance and choreography, his comments and insights usually led to long post-performance debates when we discussed such diverse aspects as the designs and lighting, the choreography and the dancers we had seen. Sometimes he was well ahead of the game when it came to booking for future productions at home and abroad. As when, several months prior to one of his planned New York trips when I thought I too might be there, he left an advance programme outside my door, listing the scheduled performances of the next New York City Ballet season at Manhattan's Lincoln Center

Dearest Alix,

Just in case you thought I was in a cataleptic trance in the car at lunchtime, I was listening to <u>your</u> radio station!

See enclosed. You can't say I don't cherish you... well, your <u>interests</u>! I imagine this Balanchine effort might be quite something. Hopefully I also will be in New York round election time – so which would you like to see! (A <u>remote</u> hope but who knows!)

Incidentally, look at those prices: 54 dollars – say, £30! No wonder the New Yorkers are planning to see "A Chorus Line" in London, England when it comes here!

Keep me in the picture, please, about THE MEN! [I was "dating" two interesting men I had recently met and he was curious as to whether either was serious boyfriend material.]

Love, H

I was also touched by his tendency to spot new books about dancers and choreographers, or classical music records, guessing, usually correctly, that these would interest me.

Dearest Alix,

This is uncannily strange. Can it be that, hidden away in the dark recesses of my psyche, is a burning yearning?

Otherwise, how do you explain that, when buying some books yesterday, I thought: "<u>Ah, Alix might like this for Christmas!</u>"

Perhaps Alix has already got it? If so, let me have it back right away as I could return it to the Baker Street shop – but

tomorrow morning. [Harold and I frequented Christopher Foss, a small independent bookshop in Baker Street, a treasure trove of recently published books.]

I've just flipped thro' it. I think it might interest even me, whom you secretly regard as fingered by philistinism.

But if you ain't got it, why, Merry Christmas! Love H

P.S. This is rather a wretched P.S. but, Alix, I've got to have that book on Dowell/Sibley [Anthony Dowell and Antoinette Sibley, at that time the major star partnership at the Royal Ballet] *back. It's not mine. Frankly, I haven't been asked for it yet (nor have I kept my promise!) So... after the jolly hols, yes. Sorry.*

Jolly hols? One thing I have done, optimist ever: ie. get fixed up now to be out of this country into a non-Christian one for next December. Year by year I swear it. Year by year I "drift" (except this time it's the "Express" following the "Mail" format that screwed my plans).

No matter how attuned I tried to be to breaking news likely to galvanise the media – forcing newspapers to change their front pages at the eleventh hour – I was sometimes unprepared when Harold had to switch plans at the last minute due to some seismic event or scandal. For him, as with most editors and journalists, work came before play. Only occasionally did he forget that rule – such as the evening he and I went to Covent Garden the night Vice-President Spiro Agnew resigned and Harold had forgotten to leave a number where he could be reached.

Among other news bombshells that forced him to cancel social engagements was the first miners' strike, Prime Minister Edward Heath's announcement of the three-day week, Watergate, the massacre of Israeli athletes at the Munich Olympic Games and the so-called 'Balcombe Street Siege', a drama that took place off Marylebone Road, not far from Portman Mansions, when a married couple were held hostage in their home by the IRA.

Equally disruptive – as in the case of Harold's note about a "cancelled Christmas" – was turbulence within Fleet Street itself. Although Harold's old newspaper, the *Daily Express*, and his present stomping ground, the *Daily Mail,* had always been traditional rivals, by the mid 1970s a long and fierce battle was being waged in Fleet Street between the two.

After a shaky start following its 1971 re-launch, with a prolonged period of teething troubles, the 'new' compact *Daily Mail* was finally beginning to hit its stride and seemed on the way to becoming the country's top selling right-wing middle market newspaper. Thanks largely to an expanding female readership and a reputation for scoops, original features and successful campaigns, circulation figures were on an upward curve. In early 1973, the paper's salacious new advertising campaign – "Every woman needs her *Daily Mail*… and every man knows why" – helped attract almost 1 million new readers within three months, overwhelmingly in the coveted high income ABC1 bracket most sought after by advertisers.

In contrast, the *Daily Express* – which once boasted the highest UK circulation at over 3.3 million – had become a melancholy shadow of its former self. Many thousands of its readers jumped ship to Rupert Murdoch's brash new *Sun* newspaper; others decamped to the *Daily Mail.* As the *Express* limped on under a series of lacklustre editors and an incompetent proprietor (Lord Beaverbrook's successor Max Aitken made it clear he knew or cared little about newspapers), the newspaper's poor layout, dull features and lack of originality drove sales further into freefall.

The financial consequences were dire. Soon, Beaverbrook Newspapers was haemorrhaging millions. Failed rebranding efforts, added to the rising cost of newsprint, industrial action by the print unions as well as constant internal strife, hirings and firings within Beaverbrook Newspapers, further cut the legs from under the once mighty organisation. There was even talk of a possible merger with the *Daily Mail.*

Finally, the *Express* decided to go tabloid like the *Mail,* and try to refashion itself as a punchy modern paper with particular appeal to women readers – an unashamed attempt to emulate the *Daily Mail.*

> *Darling Alix,*
>
> *Maybe this will please you.*
>
> *Mr Horwood* [Bill Horwood, a new features editor on Femail, who later found fame as the author of The Duncton Chronicles about a community of moles, The Book of Silence and Hyddenworld], *certainly twice in my presence, has tried to reach you. Unlike others, he is not half-heartedly enthusiastic about "Sleep" * - but (as I am and, more importantly, the Editor is) very enthusiastic.* [I had pitched an article about couples who prefer sleeping in separate beds or bedrooms to get a better night's sleep.]
>
> *Present plans are to include it in the opening days of this absolute death-or-glory, Stalingrad-style battle to crush the copycat "Express".*
>
> *Alix, my domestic affairs are sad to behold...*
>
> *Most interested to hear your news; I rang last night to see if you'd an hour to pop out. Call you.*
>
> *H*
>
> **NOT Wayne Sleep !*

Once the new-look tabloid *Daily Express* hit the newsstands, the paper's novelty value prompted an upturn in circulation. Their front page stories became splashier and more provocative, partly thanks to more book serialisations – always one of the strengths of the *Daily Mail* – and, Harold's old trick, the wholesale purchase of photographs to prevent competitors using them first. But while sales wars between the two papers continued and, briefly, the *Express* seemed as if it might give the *Mail* a run for its money, it never succeeded.

Darling Alix,

I had hoped to make contact – if that's the phrase – with you today but I tell you this: the forthcoming (March 18) "Express/Mail" confrontation is going to be a real Verdun of an encounter. We've been busy on 'tactics' all day – too long a day for my regime. (What happened to that plan NOT to go in before lunch?)

I've dropped Bernard a note which I hope he gets before he goes.

When I said "slacken the pressure", I meant on YOU: all this hot emotional paprika you find sprinkled over you: too spicy!

I can see myself missing out on Brighton YET AGAIN

Love

Harold

I usually relied on his notes to update me on his work stress, including those punishingly long hours at the newspaper. Fatigue, overwork or ill health, sometimes all three, were behind his lack of "availability". But by now I was so used to running ideas past him, even when they were not about articles for *Chandelier*, the *Grattan Mail* or the *Daily Mail*, that I unthinkingly must have added to his stress by failing to ask if the timing was convenient, or whether he was too busy to consider my questions.

I also underestimated the time and attention he devoted to reading my various projects and ideas; not for him the desultory glance and cursory thumbs-up – or down. Ideas, suggestions, proposals were digested, sometimes at length, before he responded, verbally or in writing, with valuable analysis and feedback. As with an idea I had for a weekly TV arts news programme titled *On Stage*, to be shot out and about in the West End, which would preview imminent shows or discuss and review arts events about to hit London and the South East – a bit like an on-screen *Time Out*. As usual, I sent Harold the initial pitch for approval.

Darling Alix,

*Returned as promised – with no other word until further discussion than "excellent". "On Stage" reads very well: are you having it re-typed? Do you **WANT** it re-typed?*

I really suspect you've hit on something which just hasn't thus far "made" the box. I don't know much of this medium but I know enough to be able to envisage and imagine a terrific range of visual variables if the right minds get at it.

Talking of "right minds"...

There was a new programme tonight, a sort of Kindergarten Bernard Braden, led, yes led!, by that friend of a friend called Esther Ranzen, the bee-ootiful Esther Ranzen. And among the four production "credits" at the end... who? Di Burgess! [Di was a young, former Daily Mail fashion editor whom Harold liked, and in whom she confided, broken-hearted, when her boyfriend ended their relationship.]

When we've spoken I will ring her. This must be some kind of promotion, tho I'm glad my name (or yours!) isn't on it. But that's private.

I'm sorry I didn't see until too late that you had written something on the back of your note – ie. "Le Misanthrope". My best bet for tickets is Friday. Any good? I realised too late that Wednesday is no good for me because of Watergate. TV. 10.30 onwards with John Dean under examination.

Love and good luck, Alix.

H (patient in the pad next door).

* * *

By this stage, Harold was beginning to represent a father figure to me. More than ever at the time I badly needed a steadying rock. My Russian father, whom I adored, died very suddenly a couple of months before my tenth birthday. And my Scottish stepfather, the owner of Howard & Wyndham, a major provincial and Scottish theatre empire, and of whom I was deeply fond, died when I was twenty-one. For my mother, being widowed twice within a dozen years was a crushing blow from which – especially after the loss of my stepfather, her soulmate with whom she had found great love as well as emotional and financial security – she never fully recovered.

It didn't take Freud to point out that losing two fathers in fairly rapid succession might account for my tendency to seek the friendship of comparatively older men. Occasionally, as in the case of my first serious relationship, I might also become romantically involved with someone a dozen or more years my senior.

But it was after the sudden death in the early 1970s of my beloved Czech-Russian godfather, an artist and architect as cultivated, bohemian and un-English as my father, that I realised how much I valued Harold's guidance and concern for my wellbeing. With a shock, I realised I had known Harold longer than I ever knew my father or stepfather. Now, after marking time for a dozen years, a bit-part player in my childhood, he emerged from the wings. Already my mentor, he was perfect casting for the role of surrogate father. A Yorkshireman born and raised in Dewsbury, educated in Leeds, he was thirty-four years older than me and had no children. Perhaps I represented the daughter he never had. Once we got to know one another, he was kind – and interested – enough to listen to my occasional woes about crazy flatmates or my sometimes rocky love life, which clearly puzzled him.

Because he was essentially non-judgmental and I trusted his kindness and sincerity, I felt safe enough to open up emotionally, occasionally pouring my heart out in floods of tears over some doomed relationship or unsuitable boyfriend. He was a good listener and his responses were candid. Mostly, he held up a mirror to reveal the unvarnished truth: like the extent of my denial that a relationship was heading off the tracks, or my reluctance to confront the unsuitability of some latest suitor.

Like all good therapists, he had a way of helping me distinguish fact from fantasy and see the truth for myself – much as I tried to avoid it at the time. And never did I avoid the truth more than during the break-up – more precisely a series of break-ups – with my first serious boyfriend, a divorced father of three, HR. It was a messy, occasionally bitter and drawn-out period lasting over a year and Harold was one of the few friends whom I trusted enough to take entirely into my confidence. I doubt whether he had ever come across someone as emotionally immature and self-deluded as I was at this period.

Darling Alix,

Thursday evening was a bit of an eye-opener for me. I'm flattered you gave me your confidence "in depth" (as the dreadful phrase goes) and I thought it right to let you open the old floodgates to that degree about HR.

What I hadn't realised was the secret 'fail-safe' element by which you had lived for a whole year. I'd thought the thing was more out of your system than it really was. I'd taken what you said so often at its face value, which I think you had, too, on the surface.

How can you be totally convinced that this would all not have added up to a design for disaster? The more you embroidered the picture, the more horrendous (I use the word accurately and precisely for once!) it emerged. Even the sex scenario. Believe me, I'm not a fanatical Freudian (laughter!) but that line of Tennessee Williams is true. "When a marriage goes on the rocks... the rocks are so often there in bed." Your bed was boulder-strewn before you began.

Come on now, darling. Close the chapter. Really close it. Don't pretend, which now turns out to be what you've been doing for 400 or 500 days. Too long!

Now.

Have a good party tonight.

Parties? Christ. These Christmas things: another last night: semi obligatory. And the enclosed: ditto (so do I try for the second night?).

How funny about the Dior thing. And how shrewd you are. Do you know, I'd really forgotten what I'd done with that old bottle and yet you knew. Where is it in the list ("Daily Mail" enclosed)? I'll try to find you some for Christmas.

Your record returned. On your doorstep.

I always miss you when the days slip by un-Alixed.

H

His advice to "close the chapter" I found almost impossibly hard to do. And in this particular case it was especially difficult because I had been the one to introduce HR to the woman he ended up eventually marrying. Not only was there the pain of a break-up – albeit originally initiated by me – but heaped on top of it was massively wounded pride and a profound recognition that I had brought it all on myself. The result was a prolonged plunge of self-esteem, self-inflicted mental torture and denial, even once it was patently obvious that HR had moved on and settled into a new relationship.

Darling Alix,

You said a disturbing thing the other evening. You said you hadn't got over L'Affaire HR.

None of my business - but isn't it time you had?

To be plain about the matter, you manifest signs of schizophrenia, ambivalence dichotomy - choose your own word from the current jargon vocabulary.

But the facts are there. On the one hand, you affect to hold the guy in contempt and reassure yourself that marriage to him and its consequences (quite correctly) would be a preposterous (nay, ludicrous) blunder which would blow up in your face like a hand-made IRA bomb; on the other hand, even after all this time, years which are eating away at your happiness, it pains you insufferably even to think about, to be in the same room as, the man's fiancée.

This would be understandable after a few weeks of their moving in together. But <u>after two years nearly</u>! No! It's bad. You must face what you said the other night. Wrestle with it. Expunge it. Strike it out.

If necessary you must go into analysis – but I would also fight against this with all vigour, using it only as a last resort.

But, BUT… <u>until</u> you get that man right out of your hair, your life is going to be a parade of postponements, continuously on the fringe of doing something fulfilling, forever not quite doing it.

For Christ's sake, the city is full of young men on the threshold of exciting lives and longing for a girl as attractive as you are.

Could it be – I don't mean this harshly – that you are sinking too easily back into the cocoon world of Tony Crutchley (I name this excellent fellow merely as a symbol) and thus escaping the inevitable but stimulating wrestle with your destiny?

And now you are not going to speak to me for a while – as there is nothing more odious than 'the candid friend'. But I tell you, the subconscious disclosures of the other evening depressed me.

Consult your mother – with whom you have the rare and happy capacity to be able to talk frankly because she is a wise, unembittered and philosophical person.

Next.

No go for Tuesday, I fear. Next time round for "Equus" following week. Did you by any chance see the bisexual Mr Emlyn Williams (he gave me the creeps) on the box this evening? However, high was his praise for "Equus".

Next.

Your lights were on late tonight. About one o'clock I went to the Airport Terminal for the Sunday papers; I got you a set, but when I returned only twenty minutes or so later the lights were out and I thought it best not to ring.

Take a pull, Alix. Take a pull, not a pill. I become more and more opposed to these 'pills for the mind'.

Sunday.

PS. Outside the door also is "Harpers and Queen", fatter and more prosperous than ever. Also 'your bit' of the "Sunday New York Times".

I'm not without my own problems. My ex-wife is in town and I have been seeing her quite often. So read what I've written above with this in mind. Easy to give advice to others... PPS. I shall be at the "Mail" most of the day, beginning now, 9.45

There was no question of not speaking to Harold, even for the shortest time – and he knew it. There are 'candid friends' and 'wise candid friends' and he was one of the very few whose integrity and life experience I valued sufficiently to take his advice to heart. His words, especially when committed to paper, also had the power to jolt me awake, illustrating the dismal situation as it was, not as I imagined it to be. I must have absorbed some of his wisdom by osmosis when the final missive concerning that drama arrived out of the blue a few months later, with breaking news.

Dearest Alix, 1 a.m.

You can hardly imagine I'd seen the "Express" when I

dropped a note in on you.

For the first time in months, it just wasn't delivered and no copy reached me until the office messenger arrived early evening and I've just looked at Hickey, in stupefied astonishment, JUST NOW.

Alix, I can't do anything of real help but I wish, wish, wish you'd felt able to get in touch with me. [He mistakenly thought I had already read the Express diary page in question.]

No one can do much in fact, Alix, alas, alas.

Facts are stubborn things and they have to be wrestled with; but by God, one can get roughly bruised in doing so and I've just enough perception and imagination to guess at the sheer disappointment in human behaviour when people play their hand this way: put it no higher (or lower) than that – it's so inelegant, insensitive, inept (yes, I know it's none of my business, strictly speaking, but reading that stuff cold has really rocked me).

And Jesus, I know it, the Hickeys & the Callans and all the diarists can knife you up when you're on the receiving end and not dishing it up.

That headline, that picture! But who gave them the picture? I doubt that would be in the library stock.

Call me when you feel up to it.

AND THIS TIME SCRUB THAT SLATE CLEAN – FOR GOOD

I know it's Cliché Corner to say so – but long term it's not bad news: that picture tells a terrible lot.

Come on, now......

H

He had folded a page from the previous day's *Daily Express* into the envelope and I saw at the top of the page a large 'glamour shot' of a long-haired blonde with a big smile and bare midriff. It was the actress to whom I had introduced HR two years previously. The headline, in bold type, read: *Up Pops HR with Bride* – a play on HR's publishing business which specialised in illustrated children's pop-up books. They had married the previous day nearby at Marylebone Registry Office. To my astonishment, instead of shock, fury or dismay, I felt only cool acceptance that a line had finally been drawn under a messy chapter of hysteria, jealousy, recrimination and bitterness from which no one, least of all me, came out well. Never did Harold sound so compassionate and dismayed – yet never was his dismay more unfounded.

With that episode finally over, Harold had less cause to play Freud and rescue me from despair. Other boyfriends came on the scene, stayed a while, and usually drifted off again. Mostly, those relationships were fun yet short-lived, sometimes because of what Harold saw as my skewed judgement and inability to spot some men's fear of commitment, including a tendency to rush headlong into a relationship before it had even taken off

Darling Alix,

I do worry about you a little -- especially when you are all weaponed-up for the hunt and in full cry, and judgment and sanity tend to get a <u>*teeny*</u> *bit fragmented.*

One word of advice: in that otherwise good letter (which I don't advise you have ready and therefore obviously 'pre-baked' so to speak), I'd add one thing.

Where you emphasise that you're NOT chasing him... I'd strike that bit out. Any girl who puts into writing that she's NOT chasing a man means that she IS chasing him. This is true, you know, if you think it through. It's called Department of Denials That Don't Ring True!

Good luck, my love

H

11

Last Call

BY 1976, ALTHOUGH I continued doing TV plays, including six episodes of *General Hospital* in which I played a money-grabbing divorcée trying to get her claws into an unsuspecting wealthy widower, I was beginning to get a far bigger turn-on from writing than acting.

The LBC radio work and the features commissioned by *Vogue* as well as the *Daily Mail* were more fulfilling than anything I was doing as an actress. The challenge came as much from researching, thinking through and writing these articles as it did from coming up with new ideas – or reframing old ones. More challenging still was the first hurdle: the 'pitch', trying to persuade editors why they should commission a certain piece and specifically the 'hook' which makes a story topical and relevant at that moment.

Because the idea of specialising in too narrow a subject did not appeal to me, I deliberately kept my eyes on a broad horizon, antennae tuned to all sorts of potential subjects, especially anything controversial or mildly shocking. Like the idea of a married or cohabiting couple sleeping in separate beds, or even different rooms, while maintaining a happy, fulfilled relationship.

While such apparently unorthodox sleeping arrangements were regarded as not uncommon or unnatural on the continent, in England every agony aunt and marriage guidance therapist saw sleeping 'apart' as the first step on the road to divorce. The *Daily Mail* commissioned the feature and I had fun interviewing celebrities like Katie Boyle, Hermione Gingold and the Italian wife of boxing champion Henry Cooper.

Harold was an editor ahead of his time who always thought outside the box, and encouraged all the journalists he worked with – especially women, who he thought were better at out-of-the-box thinking than men – to adopt the same left field mentality. Tuning in to emerging trends was key to getting the green light from an editor. Having one foot still in the theatre world, attending ballet and jazz dance classes to keep fit, and occasionally going to discos with friends, I got an idea which I pitched to the *Daily Mail* about how men in dance schools, companies and musicals were increasingly straight, rather than gay and therefore the image of dance as an inappropriate profession for men was changing.

The reaction was prompt and positive. Intrigued, the *Femail* editor Gerald Rudge sent me a note asking if I could change the slant to embrace non-dancers, ordinary men casting off their inhibitions on the dance floor.

Dearest Alix,

I spoke to Gerald today. He will ring you until he finds you in.

The idea sounds totally sound to me - but if it doesn't appeal to you, say so (co-operatively!) and other ideas will pop up. But this if worked out well could be good, I'd say. And bear in mind that editor David English - yes, TRUE - with his wife, is a former disco champ (only they weren't discos these many moons ago). I fool you not! David English, John Travolta and yours truly... HAROLD KEEBLE.

And, by the way, who is going to do the definitive but digestible readable piece on Lynn Seymour packing it in? [The Royal Ballet's star ballerina, Lynn Seymour, had just announced her retirement.] *That ought to be in the "Mail" but, alas, I could see it 'vapourised' on the way. Have you seen anything more than a snippet? I could well have missed it, as much preoccupied with less elevated matters. Though, if I were to tell you this week I sold a second-hand mackintosh to the widow of the President of the United States while lunching, you'd say: "He's fantasising again"... But I did. All very cosy. H*

I was delighted the *Mail* had given the story a twist. Looking back on some of my recent disco nights out, it was obvious that men, especially straight men, from all backgrounds had stopped shuffling around half-heartedly, too embarrassed and self-conscious to move freely to dance music. Their moves, like their clothes, became more flamboyant and outré and the working title for my feature was *The Peacock Brigade*.

Until then, on the dance floor, most men over about the age of thirty were like the actor Victor Spinetti who, while working as a comedian in a Soho strip club, auditioned for England's leading radical theatre director, Joan Littlewood. After his read-through, Littlewood said she wanted him to join her Theatre Workshop, but only if he worked to improve his posture, specifically his feet. "You've got apologetic feet," she told him bluntly. "Those feet have to go." And go they did, as for thousands of men around the UK, and, with the staggering success of John Travolta in *Saturday Night Fever*, the peacock revolution finally exploded and became a major world trend.

It was an intriguing subject to research, and as I was enjoying an especially hectic social life at the time, there was no shortage of men to quiz about their dancing skills. As ever, Harold was keeping half a beady eye on my entanglements and here-today-gone-tomorrow romances. As the *Sturm und Drang* of my crumbling relationship with HR finally blew over, Harold's messages and alerts reverted to their breezy, light-hearted mode. He remained amused – if baffled – by some of the boyfriends who entered, and soon exited, my life. Like someone hooked on daily TV soap operas or multi-series 'box sets', a part of him needed to be updated on changing events.

Dearest Alix,

Fascinating about Mr M! But do, I beg of you, assert your judgement. Outsiders (i.e. me!) don't really know, but on the surface someone who says he is half homosexual and can't have children might seem a little less than par for the course as a husband. But you know... I don't.

What I'd hate to see though, is you in another muddle. I sincerely mean this.

Love, H

He needn't have worried. I was having fun, going out with several different people and, although flattered that one or two seemed quite smitten, I was finally beginning to recognise when a 'type' of man – like Mr M, a divorcee who nonetheless confessed to the occasional gay encounter in his early youth – was unsuitable long-term material.

Later on, things got a bit more serious when I met another '*beau*', although not for long. For a few months, to earn some spare cash, I took a part-time job in Selfridge's, demonstrating a new 'mix and match' perfume business where a resident chemist blended unique, bespoke perfumes for individual customers, mixing specific raw ingredients while they waited. My 'boss' at Parfums Le Jardin was a tall, silver-haired Canadian ex-model with whom I got on well, and who I assumed was gay. After a few platonic dates together and a boozy dinner on my birthday, the silver fox, as I came to think of him, asked me to marry him.

He was divorced and had a grown-up daughter in Canada

whom he rarely saw or talked to. But, as dishy, intelligent and amusing as he was, I saw from the outset that his private life was a mess and he seemed prone to depression. Although I was fond of him and it was flattering to be proposed to, instinctively I suspected it was unlikely to happen. For one thing, he had booked a trip to South Africa and planned after that to go on to the US as he had grown tired of London. Proposing marriage a fortnight before boarding a long-distance flight did not augur well and suggested a feeble sense of commitment. Besides, I was past the stage of chasing men who played hard to get.

Alix:

Marriage In the Fall? Has the recent heat deranged you?

I must know more.

But of course I'm delighted (if you are).

Remember this tho'! The only reason for getting married is that life would be unthinkable without him.

You set me a hard one on "A Chorus Line" first night. I doubt you've any idea how hard - but just sometimes (via the "Sunday Times") I have luck.

Now, wedding presents... where do I start?

H

Harold had never met the silver fox. But someone he knew did and obviously reported back to him.

Alix:

SUFFICE IT TO SAY *that the "pretty girl" you mention said, somewhat infuriatingly, of the person getting out of the lift: "what an attractive man!" And this is TRUE; no con! (Somewhat "infuriatingly"... No, not really... This is a very wistful old gentleman who addresses these words to you...) Obviously I read the phrase... "my husband before 1976 is* *out" with eye-popping interest – you know I do. More please. Fewer broad brush strokes; more detail!*

SUFFICE IT TO SAY *I'm bloody sorry meanwhile about the USA cock-up: I had thought you'd hopped it! Internal travel in the States is fairly cheap but not that cheap, I'd have thought: I'll ask tonight. You do appreciate that the Bicentennial Bonanza is making America this year a bit like a non-stop Cup Final.*

SUFFICE IT TO SAY *that if you are delayed briefly, I would like you to do a short (500 word) interview with Italian designer Piatelli* [Bruno Piatelli had recently become a 'hot' fashion designer, principally of men's clothes and the first person to introduce male fashion models to the catwalk] *in the next five days. Not for the "Mail". But fee £35 only. Sometime Monday or Tuesday, probably.*

H

Eighteen months later, I was walking through New York's Times Square and ran into the silver fox. For some extraordinary reason, when I got to New York I had a premonition that I would see him there unexpectedly. Although we shared some fun outings and he poured his heart out to me, sometimes dissolving into floods of tears, we parted as good friends. And never saw one another again.

From Harold's brief reference to the 'USA cock-up', I knew that he was disappointed by my decision to cancel a previous trip to New York I had planned for a while. Being a man for whom thought was action, he took a dim view of people who hesitated too long when making decisions, or did not follow through with existing plans. As he made clear after I cancelled another New York trip scheduled several months later.

Dear Alix,

Though it's an intrusion to say so, you are foolish again to postpone again your visit to the States: it is a mistake – that country is more (not less) interesting than ever. There is a danger in developing into 'A Postponement Person' (I speak from experience! Tho', mostly, if I say I'm going, I go).

Come on now! Look in and see me. Maybe we both need to be 'sorted out'!

H

Since it was often money – or lack of it – that led me to cancel travel plans, once I added up the amount I needed for air fares, hotels and sundries, it rankled with me that he saw me as privileged, a woman with few concerns about money, possibly with a private income, all of which was far from the truth.

Having started earning money in my mid teens, paid for my theatrical 'digs' and travel and managed all other expenses, I was always acutely aware of the need to live within my means and stick to a strict budget. Saving money and finding bargains was a constant obsession. I loathed asking my mother for money, and rarely did so. This was a legacy of my childhood and the often frightening financial poverty that kept my parents up late, arguing and agonising throughout the night over how to pay the rent and the week's food bill.

Fear of poverty never left me entirely and it taught me a crucial lesson in being 'sensible' with money. The job I took at Selfridges for Parfums Le Jardin was chiefly to reassure myself that if ever I couldn't get work in show business or through writing, I could earn a living working in the glamour end of retail, no matter how physically exhausting, mind-numbingly dull and monotonous the job.

Therefore when the odd acquaintance commented on me being "privileged", "spoilt", "not having to worry" or, worse still, a "dilettante" who didn't need to work, my hackles rose instantly. As when Harold remarked in a note, after I wrote to him that I lacked sufficient funds to go on a particular foreign trip.

Dearest Alix,

Old catch-phrases sponged down for use again....

WHEN I READ YOUR NOTE ABOUT THE FINANCIALLY-IMPOSED DELAY ... "You have to be joking!"

Love Harold

This was soon followed by another breezy assessment of my finances.

Dear Alix,

I'm anxious to get this little matter [an article he asked me to write] *off the ground so I'll give you a call until I reach you and we'll just run through what has to be done. Give it a look over anyway: I'll probably do a bit in that NEWS DESK section which I might get you interested in too, if ever small numbers of £s concern you. I always regard you really as sailing imperiously above the squalor of pounds and pence.*

H

When I eventually told him that I had to keep an eagle eye on my expenses, he got the message.

Dear Alix,

Positively...

The last exchange (present series only!) of notes!

I am sorry. In view of what you vigorously say, I rather regret what I put in that note. Truly I didn't mean it that way - as a rebuke: rather encouragement to action as I always envisage you as a hyper-active person.

Tough luck!

But I know that (with certain exceptions and I'm lucky there) - you've got it wrong about my financial unconcern over travel fares! When are they going to stop?

Molly (Lady Daubeny to you!) wants me to go to South Africa next month. So do I. Fare: £1,040. And I'll tell you this: the fare to Leeds (let alone Hong Kong) LEEDS is £23.40. I have a ticket to prove it.

No, m'love. I'm urging all the young chicks I know (like you) to get moving, get your skates on before it's £100 to get from Dover to Calais.

Drink this evening?

Or are you going to the Ritz where I went last night – there were ten people in the restaurant.

Lies, of course – what they say! The Ritz is doomed, just as Prunier's closed last week.

Long Live Leyland Motors and Merrie England

H

* * *

I WAS ALWAYS delighted when Harold asked me out of the blue to write an article, as he did with the Bruno Piatelli piece, or when he mentioned that one of the *Daily Mail* editors was enthusiastic about a subject I had suggested or just written for the paper. The more I divided my time and energies between acting and journalism, the more I felt myself being nudged towards a crossroads where I knew eventually I would have to make a definite choice: newspapers or show business.

The crunch came unexpectedly, with preparations for the London production of the smash Broadway hit *A Chorus Line*, due to be staged the following year at the Theatre Royal, Drury Lane. Donna McKechnie, whose dance role in the musical *Promises, Promises* I had taken over in 1968, had achieved a huge personal success in the central role of Cassie, which won her a Tony award as Best Actress in a Musical and made her an overnight star. Donna was now the toast of Broadway, and auditions were being held in London to find British dancer-actors for the West End production.

My agent got me an audition; it turned out to be a primary 'cattle call' attended by scores of dancers, to weed out those lacking a strong jazz style and technique. It had been many years, probably since my teens, since I attended one of these mass auditions and as I joined the throng crowding onto the stage at Drury Lane, I could feel all my very early teenage feelings of powerlessness and inadequacy welling up inside.

Surrounded by dozens of dancers, I stood in the wings waiting to go on and perform first a ballet combination and then a hastily learnt section of the show's opening jazz routine, which we all performed in groups of six. The problem wasn't learning the routine or performing it – that was easy for me and I knew I did it well, without nervousness. Instead, what hit me square-on was the symbolism and meaning of this audition – for this show particularly – in my own life.

The show is about a group of young male and female dancers auditioning for a new musical and being asked to lay bare all their fears, insecurities and dreams to the choreographer-director, who remains a disembodied voice at the back of the stalls and is ultimately responsible for hiring or dismissing them.

This very scenario – with the exception of any soul-baring – was exactly what every one of us on the stage was going through for real that day. There was no empowerment for the male and female artists, who included youngsters just out of dance school alongside experienced stage and TV performers and also dancers well into middle-age, hoping to reboot a flagging career. Just like the character in the show, the choreographer-director holding the audition held the ultimate power to promote and build a dancer's future or, by rejecting them, perhaps crush their confidence or shred their hopes and aspirations.

Although I came through that first round and was recalled to another audition in a few days' time, I never went back. Suddenly, the theatre, a world of which I had been a part since childhood, had lost its magic and allure. Fleet Street, less than half a mile from Drury Lane, was now where I wanted to be. It was where I had already dipped a toe and felt both confident and accepted.

A Chorus Line was the last audition I attended and I never regretted not going back.

Several months later, the London production of *A Chorus Line* went into rehearsals, only to make headlines with an unexpected behind-the scenes fracas which played out very publicly. The long-established actress-dancer Elizabeth Seal, who made her name in British musicals in the 1950s and 1960s and won a Tony award for her role in *Irma La Douce* on Broadway, was cast to play the part of Cassie, Donna McKechnie's role, in the West End.

About three-quarters of the way through rehearsals, the show's creator, director-choreographer Micheal Bennett, whom I knew from my work in *Promises, Promises*, suddenly and unceremoniously sacked her, allegedly on the grounds that she wasn't suited to the role. Michael was a brilliant, innovative artist and undoubtedly had sound reasons to 'let her go'. But, for an artist of Elizabeth Seal's reputation, it was a bitter and humiliating blow, especially at this stage in her career.

But the drama had only begun. There followed a couple of weeks' headlines as Michael Bennett – who, after the Broadway success of *A Chorus Line*, married Donna McKechnie, his muse, collaborator and closest friend since both were in their teens – went to war with British Equity, the actors union. Bennett wanted Donna to open the London production in her role of Cassie and continue performing until a suitable replacement could take over the role.

Initially, Equity gave permission for Donna to perform in London; but shortly afterwards they revoked the decision and banned her from joining the show. For several days Donna – who had arrived in London to join Michael – made the front pages as the battle with Equity continued. When Equity refused to budge, Elizabeth Seal's understudy, dancer Petra Siniawski, was hastily promoted to play the role of Cassie.

Such a farrago seemed to me another illustration of how, especially in musicals, talented performers, many of them seasoned pros with a track record, could be manipulated or sidelined according to a director's whims and backstage politics. Naturally, given the world of show business, in cases like this, no financial compensation was either sought by an artist, or awarded by the production company. Sackings, loss of earnings, public humiliation, came with the territory – unless you were lucky enough to be a major star. Of course, it was ever thus in the world of theatre – with the sole exception of musicians, whose union is one of the strongest and most militant in the entertainment industry – but that didn't make it any less unedifying.

Some months on, however, I had great fun interviewing some leading West End dancers for my LBC programme on what they thought of the show's message: that dancers are motivated primarily by passion and a deep love of their art and will therefore endure injuries, low pay, punishing work schedules, exhaustion, as well as frequently being bullied and demeaned by directors, choreographers and producers, simply to be able to dance for the sheer joy of it. But by far the happiest outcome of my then very faint acquaintance with Donna McKechnie, was that when we met again years later, she became one of my dearest close friends.

I never for a moment regretted that moment of truth on the Drury Lane stage. Quite the opposite. A burden had been lifted from my shoulders and, recognising the opportunity I was given to reinvent myself, I saw clearly the path ahead.

Having set off along that path, I had to accept that my early ambition to become a dance critic was a non-starter. Despite the challenge of my regular LBC gigs, there were massive obstacles to breaking into print. Newspaper and magazine dance critics were impossible to topple from their perch: they seemed to inhabit hallowed ground. None voluntarily left their jobs, and if they did it was usually just to swap one publication for another. I did manage to write several dance previews and reviews for a new glossy magazine called *Boulevard*, founded and edited by a wealthy and colourful young entrepreneur, 'Baron' Stephen Bentinck, a relative of the billionaire art collector and museum founder Baron Heini Thyssen. Bentinck was frequently dubbed the 'Bonkers Baron' in gossip columns, on account of his habit of lavishing vast sums on his publishing and other businesses which, as did *Boulevard,* crashed spectacularly

Somewhere between exercise, fitness and the burgeoning field of 'alternative medicine' and 'holistic healthcare', which claimed to offer effective alternatives to conventional medicine, another sphere of wellbeing was opening up in the UK: self-improvement systems promising to change self-destructive behaviour and banish negative thinking. Several of my friends had paid vast sums of money to take such courses, and came away raving about the benefits. Unfortunately, they also attempted to persuade non-believers like myself to take part, affecting an almost evangelical zeal normally associated with followers of dangerous cults and organised religions.

As with my refusal to try drugs, I always avoided being drawn into any so-called New Age philosophies, Eastern practices and mind-altering techniques. What disturbed me was that friends who got involved in the newest self-improvement programme or system ended up becoming insufferably smug and patronising, even aggressive, towards those like myself who had not tried it. Instead of broadening their world and making them more tolerant of other views, these proselytisers became frighteningly blinkered and dogmatic.

Of course, I recognised the rich potential of these philosophies to make colourful copy. Through a friend and former fellow dancer, Don McLennan, I had been introduced to a form of Japanese Buddhism called Nichiren Shoshu, which Don had been practising and described to me in refreshingly non-esoteric, down-to-earth terms. In fact, the most surprising thing about Nichiren Shoshu was the complete absence of any psychobabble or airy-fairy mysticism. This alone made it stand out among the surrounding clamour – it didn't even identify itself as a self improvement movement.

Apparently, most adherents had been persuaded of its powers by initially chanting for material things such as a new home, a job, or even money. In fact, that was its Unique Selling Point. You didn't have to renounce worldly goods to become this type of Buddhist and the practice was relatively simple and undemanding. Practitioners merely chanted one simple phrase repeatedly for fifteen minutes twice a day – "Nam-Myoho-Renge-Kyo" – while visualising the thing they desired. Many claimed that within weeks or months of chanting, they found some means of attaining their wish. Strangely, Nichiren Shoshu had at that stage received no press coverage in the UK, despite its popularity among celebrities including the singers Sandie Shaw, Tina Turner, Boy George and fashion PR Lynne Franks

Around the same time, a buzz was developing around the practices developed by a jolly, fat little Indian called Bagwan Shree Rajneesh, who was beginning to acquire a following among Westerners travelling to India in search of self-enlightenment. He appeared to have set himself up as a rival to the already famous Indian guru to the stars, Maharishi Mahesh Yogi, whose devotees included the Beatles and other world-famous entertainers.

I heard that one of Bagwan's practices, 'Dynamic Meditation', practised in the nude, had gained popularity in the UK and was being held around London, in people's attics, studios and basements. These dervish-like events, where practitioners were encouraged to over-breathe, moan, bellow and scream while shaking and rolling naked around on the floor, were followed by talks, pre-recorded on audio-tape by the Bagwan in a wispy little voice, on the merits of freeing mind and body of daily stresses.

As with Nichiren Shoshu, the cult of Bagwan Rajneesh was too good a story to miss, especially since no one so far had written about it. Instead of approaching the *Daily Mail* or any other newspaper, I contacted BBC Radio's *Woman's Hour*, which at the time was commissioning work from freelancers. I was invited into the *Woman's Hour* offices to talk the idea over with the producer and managed to convince him I had plenty of interviewees lined up, all with varying points of view

More to the point, these practices, with their repertoire of Japanese phrases and chanting on the one hand and outpouring of primal orgiastic sounds on the other – plus the Baghwan, who talked in a sibilant half-whisper – were tailor-made for the medium of radio. He liked the idea and dispatched me to the bowels of Broadcasting House to collect an old-fashioned, heavy-duty tape recorder called a Uher, used by all roving radio reporters at the time. After half an hour's tuition from a BBC technician on how to operate the Uher, I was off to record my programme.

There was no problem finding enough lively, articulate practitioners of Nichiren Shoshu – including Richard Causton, a sober-suited Englishman with a Japanese wife, who studied it while working in Tokyo and founded the first UK branch. Devotees of Bagwan Rajneesh were also eager to talk on radio about their experiences, though they tended to use more New Age jargon to praise the guru and his teachings.

The most impressive part of the soundtrack was the cacophony of one of their Dynamic Meditation sessions which I recorded in Islington. There, two dozen naked men and women writhed, rolled and leapt about, panting and groaning, on the floor of a hot, sweaty basement, so foul-smelling it became difficult to breathe without gagging.

The programme turned out to be lively, controversial and provocative – but there was one missing item. Jean Mann, an American journalist friend, also pitched an idea to *Woman's Hour* about a new generation of druids making waves on the New Age circuit. The producer suggested Jean and I combine our various segments and hand our tapes in together. The working title for the three segments was Alternative Religions and the producer seemed pleased with our efforts and told us the programme would go out several weeks after he finished editing.

As I listened to the feature on Radio Four, to my alarm it consisted only of my interviews and voice-overs: Jean's druids had landed on the cutting room floor. I was mortified, especially because she had experienced difficulties in recording her interviews. The druids she finally recorded provided only halting or incoherent comments. As our producer discovered, druids don't make good interviewees.

When I phoned her to commiserate, I could tell she suspected that I, not the producer, might be responsible for cutting her contribution. We never discussed it again and it was a few years before she and I met again as friends.

12

Between The Lines

When a man takes on the role of mentor, confidant and father figure to a much younger woman, the frequent assumption is that they must be having an affair. Or that one of them, usually the man, hopes they will. Especially where the man in question admits loving the company of women, especially ones who are bright, confident and good-looking – not that I actually believed I possessed any of those attributes. In the case of Harold and me, any romantic or sexual entanglement could not have been further from the truth. Quite the contrary. I believe it is because Harold never once attempted to make a pass at me during twelve years of close friendship that our relationship worked so well. As he wrote after an enjoyably relaxed weekend at his home in Brighton…

Dearest Alix,

If it wasn't so late I'd whipper-upper a little something as Merman belts of "Gypsy".

Thanx for all (so welcome!) on my doorstep, including

the nice invitation from your mum and the nice things you say about the two or three days just past.

The last bit I'm rather sorry about – maybe. First, there's no need to drop me (however well said) a note of 'thank you'; and second, I'd rather hoped to drop you a note, saying the same thing ahead of you. BRIGHTON, week-ending July 25-27th, was a strictly non-directional, strictly underplanned and without much – (much? any!) social buoyancy. But for my part, anyway, I really felt we could talk a lot or not talk a lot, vanish from the room or stay in it, pop back to London and return (either of us) and all the time there was just no tension in the wires, none at all. It was great your being there; and I wanted to say so. Amen.

About all other things (Munich put back one more day due to Reginald Maudling) shall we really talk in the morning? H

It was a perfect summary of a laid back July weekend spent in harmony. Two friends completely at ease with one another, with so much to talk and laugh about that, when silence did occasionally fall, it floated spontaneously and naturally. The rapport between us reflected the extraordinary extent to which we were on the same wavelength when it came to many mutual interests – music, theatre, current affairs, publishing, travel and more.

Dear young Miss K,

We really get on very well together, you and I, you know. I appreciate that, from time to time, you want to spit in my eye (for example when the tearsheet on your Piatelli article is mislaid); but 'au fond' – yes definitely, AU FOND! – we 'make our poem rhyme', to adjust Mr James Webb (?) a little...

And, if you want a lesson in how to write with deceptive

ease (packing the facts in among the style), you might even look at the enclosed. There could, seriously, hardly be any subject or a man who to interest you less – but this effortless polish is WHY Ian Wooldridge gets the award as the best newspaper writer of the year: not just on sport and the redoubtable Eddie, either. [The Ian Wooldridge article he included here was about the popular Yorkshire sports personality from Harold's home town of Dewsbury, Eddie Wareing.]

Eddie, for Christ's sake! Why do I battle for Eddie? ANSWER: Because he's genuine – genuinely ghastly!

Remember 'our song': "People who need people are the ghastliest people in the world!"

You're in great form, Miss K!

H

PS. You don't have any portable kennels, do you? As I'm currently in the dog-house with: Miss M; "The Daily Mail"; Miss L; V.A.T; Alfa-Romeo; The Inland Revenue; – but NOT your mum, who made a most kind suggestion to me.

Given our similar tastes and interests, it didn't surprise me when Harold gave me books and articles as examples of fine writing, but covered subjects he guessed rightly would intrigue me. The same applied to music. One evening, I discovered outside my door an empty beige double album cover of recordings by Bobby Short, an American singer and pianist of whom I had never heard. It wasn't long before I became hooked on this quintessential New Yorker's husky voice and unique keyboard style. Ever since then, Bobby Short, whom I later managed to see in cabaret at Manhattan's Carlyle Hotel, has remained one of my favourite jazz artists.

Darling Alix,

A few sundry items for you. If you waken before 2pm please give me a ring.

I've just received an LP from New York, a double LP (from Susan actually!) which is very much 'you'. A dozen little-known Cole Porter numbers. Call in, and listen to my etchings -in stereo on wax! Case enclosed. Christ, these are virtually rejected numbers and they're better than your Sondheim and Lennon successes! I'll have them taped for you. At last I've got these tape systems in action here!

I've talked to your mother this evening – maybe I'll talk to you tomorrow.

Love

H

Apart from books, music, theatre and journalism, foreign travel was another passion which Harold and I shared, although at the time he had ample business reasons and opportunities to travel and the countries he visited were usually more exotic and remote than those on my typical European itinerary. Other people's travel plans were always a constant source of interest and good-natured envy for me and there were times when he outlined some stupendously exciting foreign schedule that prompted me to tease him about coming along "to carry your pencils".

Sometimes, when he had a relatively short-haul trip coming up, such as Paris or Munich, where he went to investigate the city's preparations for the 1972 Olympics, I would share my own knowledge if I knew a city well, as I did Paris and Munich. Since my mother first took me, aged four, to Paris to stay with her sister, I had visited Paris often from my early twenties on, both for work and pleasure. I also visited Munich several times as a child to stay with my aunt and uncle, returning later as an adult to visit the galleries and museums. Swapping stories about places inevitably led us to conjecture whether we would make good travel companions. At one point, when it seemed we might both be in Paris at the same time, a note suggested it would be fun if we had an opportunity to meet there for lunch.

It would be nice to mesh gears in the Paris timetable. Hey – "block that metaphor" as we say on the "New Yorker".

When he wrote to me during his visits to Munich, Egypt, Kenya, Hong Kong and New York, his letters fizzed with the excitement and energy of those places and I realised he would have been the perfect person to introduce me to them. And he knew it, too.

Dear Alix

Many thanx for your generous note: I'm very sincere. I would have answered it earlier, only Queenie put it on the table in the passage, someone else put something on top of it – and I didn't see it until fairly late.

Re Very Important Pharaohs, the Nile, Abu Simbel and that gang: very privately to you, the thought had crossed my mind – only I'm fundamentally a very shy Yorkshireman! (Some people don't believe this.)

It would be marvellous from my view on the bridge, because my blood or bones or whatever tell me we get on pretty well together.

Only... how can I wish for something which is dependent on your ***NOT*** *getting something you've set your heart on! (The 'mystery lady' is no 'mystery' but a slight problem of the conscience: I'll explain.)*

Delighted about the weekend. I'll ring you to fix a time that suits you best; and, secondly, dependent on whether I have to work Sunday, which I'll know this morning.

Re enclosed: Aren't people extraordinary! Imagine hand-stitching say 500 of these! [A newspaper spread about a spectacular evening dress shown at the Paris collections, designed by Norman Hartnell, made of appliqued beads, pearls and other semi precious jewels on silk.] *And I haven't seen Norman for about 10 years! I knew him when the Express used to do scoops on the monarch's clothes.*

Take care

Harold

Although my jaunty asides about accompanying him to carry his pencils were made in jest, sometimes the remarks were more serious. And as time went on, I realised that he wasn't always able to tell the difference. The real problem was, neither did I, since I kept changing my mind when it came to travel.

As when he first chided me for cancelling a trip to New York, he was utterly unaware of my frequent nervousness about booking long-haul trips and the major anxiety that accompanied any such travel plans. I suspected the root cause of my 'travel anxiety' went back a long way, probably to childhood, and was always more nerve-racking when there were emotional dramas playing out in my life. As a result, I tended to invent reasons why an upcoming trip should be postponed or cancelled, dreaming up imaginary obstacles like a social event, a friend's birthday, a planned visit to the theatre, or something else unlikely to deter others from travelling abroad.

I think all my fear and hesitancy over whether to book a trip – and then stick to a travel plan – was subconsciously associated with the very real separation anxiety I first developed as a child after my father's death. From that time, my mother's profession as a theatrical costumier required her to travel to Scotland and other parts of England when dress rehearsals and the opening of a new show demanded her presence as part of the production team. I dreaded those times, when I would develop a sense of impending doom, convincing myself that something terrible would happen to my mother or to me while she was away, leaving me alone in London in the care of an au pair, or with the parents of school friends who put me up in their home.

Such apprehension about travel was always far worse on the days before a trip – whether I or my mother was the one travelling. Once she or I had arrived at a destination, all fear evaporated and I felt perfectly relaxed. But poor Harold didn't know that. Since I never explained my intense 'pre-travel' phobia and tendency to chop and change plans, sometimes even cancelling a journey a day or two before travelling, he merely saw me as wholly unreliable, neurotically dithering over plans until the last moment. Nor did it help that I hated flying and would be in a state of panic about an impending long-haul flight.

This was what happened with Harold's business trip to Egypt, a country I had always wanted to visit and a journey I was longing to share with him.

> *Dear, dear Alix,*
>
> *Super Calamity! Having no news of you, I 'wrote off' tonight.* [I had bought theatre tickets and invited him, but inexplicably we failed to confirm the date earlier in the day.] *Additionally, for a change, there have been some upheavals for me personally. However, apart from being dismally disappointed (I love going to the theatre with you) clearly you must not be out of pocket. Here therefore, with wretched apologies, is the money for the tickets.*
>
> *Next.*
>
> *Things move fast at Northcliffe House. And, for me, it is now or never to get away.*
>
> *I've fixed to go tomorrow 7.30. And I'm heartily unhappy about the arrangements. I still haven't got my visa (one forgets how basically hostile Egypt is to newspapers) and believe it or not there is no telephone communication with Cairo without 2 hours delay so I've no hotel, either. However I'm seeing the First Secretary at the Embassy at 5 o'clock and he "promises me" etc., etc. I have got a flight on Japanese Airlines.*

Of course, if I make it and you'd still like to wander up the Nile – well, Alix, I'd love it if you'd join me and I'd try to make some effort to take your mind off matters which really occupy you, ie. Bickenhall Mansions. [A boyfriend with whom I had recently broken up lived in Bickenhall Mansions.] *Be honest now, two days in Paris is one thing. Luxor takes you very far away.*

There at the bottom of the page, he added a boxed-off footnote, in blue ink, not brown like the rest of the letter:

You must understand that with all your 'could-be, couldn't-be appointments', all my instincts told me: "this is a non-starter".

Next, though. If you have a minute, when I surface, I would like to sort out that Beauty piece and the next one for "Chandelier". I'll call you to see if you could make a drink just before lunch or sometime later. Not least of my irritating problems is that I've lost my vaccination certificate!

Oh hell.

And oh hell about tonight – but you did vanish, dear Alix, did you not?

See you, please.

Love

Harold

Of course he was right. My private life was too riddled with complications, not to mention panic attacks, every time I seriously considered booking a flight to Cairo to join Harold in Egypt. I too knew it was never going to happen.

I soon spotted that once he embarked on a trip on which there was a possibility I might join him, in his letters, hovering among the general news and observations, was the merest hint, a furtive aside, that he would have enjoyed my company.

Hotel Kempinski Berlin

Dear, dear, very dear Alix,

Don't think I'd like to live here.

But been having (except for one missing ingredient!) an absolutely absorbing time in wonderful, wonderful Munich, whither I hope to return tonight. So much going on!

Mind you, it's not exactly 'Bargainsville' where all the action is! (The so-called Olympic 'village' is beyond belief!)

My seat (normal price, no black market stuff) for "Eugen Onegin" was nearly £13. I reckon with the mark at under 7 to the £, you or I could take a couple of friends to a good dinner and four seats at the National Theatre (as they call this breathtaking opera house) and have change out of £100.

The hotel, which is superb (so actually was Hamburg), runs along these financial lines which in fact will soon have to bring me back.

I've tried telephoning. I'll try again. I do want to hear good news of you and how I'd love to hear it personally here... well not 'here', but in good old München. I miss you, childishly maybe... H

Sometimes, even when he was in a country such as Kenya that held less appeal for me, I sensed he was imagining what his sojourn might have been like if I had been on the trip. Even if he was perhaps comparing me to the person he was actually there with, whose identity he did not divulge.

NEW STANLEY HOTEL, NAIROBI

Darling Alix,

Many many thanx for your warming (this is an M) letter, though it left me a little intrigued and puzzled. Reason I couldn't reply – will explain later.*

It has been an unsteady and disturbing trip.

While I have been creating problems for myself, I hope you've been solving yours.

How different it would have been had you been there. Yes, how different.

See you around. Today? Except that I can hardly see through bleary eyes.

Love H

I knew that our friendship was on an intimate footing when he began occasionally to ask me over for supper at his flat instead of going to a restaurant. To me, being invited to "take pot luck" at home – even though he usually had his housekeeper, Queenie, or part-time chauffeur, Durban, rustle up dinner and serve it in his dining room – was one of the most flattering of compliments, genuine confirmation of how comfortable he felt in my company.

On such occasions, he might spontaneously order in a simple, luxurious meal, like dressed crab, one of his favourites because he loved the ease of eating it without having to tangle with shells, joints and claws to get at the meat. As a seafood lover, he frequently ordered choice delicacies to be delivered by our local fishmonger. Blagden's of Paddington Street, at the top of Chiltern Street, was no ordinary fishmonger, but a long established institution, 'By Appointment to Her Majesty The Queen', which sold fine, ready-prepared fish, game, bouillabaisse and shellfish of the finest quality and at prices equivalent to Harrod's Food Hall.

When it came to dining, Harold loved classic dishes of the highest quality and simplicity, and always returned to the classiest traditional shops and restaurants. Travelling back together by train from my first stay with him in Brighton, he told me he had some excellent smoked salmon at home which he invited me to share, and insisted on pre-ordering a starter of lobster bisque from Prunier's in St James's, one of London's most exclusive fish restaurants.

Because he had an urgent phone call to make at home, he dropped me off by taxi at Prunier's to collect the bisque and bring it home. While I waited in the curtained lobby for the food to arrive, Madame Prunier, the legendary diminutive French founder of the restaurant, got chatting and gave me precise instructions on the correct way to heat up the lobster bisque using a bain-marie – a double saucepan containing hot water beneath to warm up the ingredients in the receptacle above.

"Mademoiselle, you must be very careful zat you do not allow ze water to boil too long. If you let eet bubble too long, zees veel 'eat ze soup too fast and make it boil! Remember, ze bisque must nevair boil, it must not get too 'ot, or it veel be ruined. Lentement! Doucement, gentle, gentle, eet must re'eat slowly in ze bain-marie. Zen it veel be perfect!" Suitably coached by the doyenne of seafood, I returned to Portman Mansions for our slap-up fish supper.

Hi, little friend,

I shall meet you, I hope, tonight, with a cheque!

But, Alix, you do know the situation I'm in - and would it be OK if Durban simply gave us supper (I have to have someone in here from Nairobi about 7.30 briefly). This scrappy social life I'll try to make up to you on (or if!) my return from Africa. I truly will. [This was another of his visits to Africa.]

Now... the Voice of the Tempter in the Land...

You're not going to NY, are you ? [Another trip to New York was hanging in the balance.]

WHY? Why should you?

The nicer things are here. Every nightmare aspect of 'the doomed city' will be multiplied (every inconvenience compounded) by the election run-up.

If you have a real purpose, my advice is "Yes". If not...

well, do police-guarded subways in the city with the worst transport system in the world really "call" you?

I joke a little.

It is the Voice of the Tempter in the Land... speaking selfishly because he'd miss you.

I'll ring you

And thanx for the specs.

Love

Harold

You didn't have to read too closely between the lines to guess that, with subtlety, tact and nuance, he was testing the waters. Writing about pending or current foreign trips, he always let a sliver of light escape a closed door, keeping our options open. Although I often assumed he wasn't interested, probably because he had ample problems of his own – I presumed these were often associated with women in his life – he must have thought better about risking the end of a special friendship by trying to seduce an immature twenty-something with a bumpy private life, lugging a sackful of emotional baggage. After all, if that went wrong, who would pick up the pieces?

Eventually, a letter arrived from Hong Kong, crackling with enthusiasm: however, for the first time it contained no reference to my absence. I sensed a subtle gear change.

The Mandarin
Hong Kong

Dearest Alix,

So you see! Always ahead of the pack - even the Chinese pack!

I had no conception of what an incredible city this has become: its electrifying urgency (I have the added and ego-massaging asset of access to a private helicopter); and visually – especially at night; more stunning than any city I've ever been in (possible exception, Rio).

Went to Manila in the Philippines over the weekend; like Macau island (ten minutes from this superb hotel by helicopter), Manila very tricky; very Tennessee Williams territory.

I don't escape the weather however: two typhoons – but warm sunny days between.

Been here longer than I intended – much longer.

Possible return with stopover Bangkok and Teheran.

Love, H

PS. Maybe I'll regret to the end of my days that I never once married an elegant Chinese girl... so unlike the Japanese.

Could he be grappling with new complications in his personal life? Had someone special come onto the scene? There was little opportunity to find out because he was soon on the move again, taking extended trips to the Far East and Africa, apparently travelling as much for pleasure as for work. Which explained why we saw little of each other for several months.

Dearest Alix,

One of the novels (I forget which) by the late great Raymond Chandler begins with the terrific line: 'They went to bed as friends – and woke up strangers'.

While hardly claiming this has much relevance to our lives (!) it is nonetheless astonishing how not just days or weeks, but months can go by, living next door, and never even running into each other.

What about, also, your friend I promised to see? [This was Jean Mann, the journalist and wife of Robin Lang's friend John Morton, whose druid interviews were cut from the Woman's Hour programme on which we collaborated.]

Since getting back from S.E Asia I've been under a bit of pressure, but maybe the curve is straightening out a bit (foolish, headstrong optimism!).

So, if agreeable, let's really, REALLY try to set up something next week before unthinkable Christmas is upon us!

Love, YOUR FRIENDLY NEIGHBOUR

Several months after the end of Harold's globe-trotting schedule, I got hold of tickets to the press night of a new Tom Stoppard play, and found he too had tickets for the same performance. However, he later confided that he had to return them to the box office because the person he was going with had backed out. I didn't see a problem: the solution seemed obvious; he would come to the premiere with me, I said, and left it at that.

Early the next morning, however, I found a note under my door which, even with what *Daily Mail* Editor David English described as 'Keeble's capacity for chaos', hit new heights of melodrama.

Darling Alix,

Obviously you won't believe this – but there are periods of my life when all engines seem to be running fairly sweetly – but you, poor Alix, don't hear much about 'em!

I must be frank – I am very disappointed about this. It was one first night I did want to go to; and in the end the tickets were a nightmare to get.

Doubly infuriating is the fact that I AM ACTUALLY FREE TO GO – and, by golly, would be honoured indeed – I truly mean this – to be your escort.

However...

Dept. of High Drama

Has taken over.

To encapsulate long story: person I was taking has been prevented – (oh yes, Dept of High Drama all right!) 'prevented'/FORBIDDEN I mean – and she's in a terrible state.

(AH, THAT FAMILIAR SCENARIO... WHY DON'T I PACK IT IN! BASKET CASE THAT I AM!) And I do care about her rather a lot & it would hurt her if I took someone else (maybe someone quite so stunning as you – she's seen you... you haven't seen her...) etc., etc. and so on and so forth. (Enough, Keeble, Cut! End message.)

Hope you enjoy it. Will positively be in touch Thursday. Won't be available tomorrow... Love HAROLD

Finally, the mist began to clear. Someone special had stepped into his life. But, on top of all the usual work pressures and serious ups and downs of his health, he now, obviously, had also got his love life into a terrible tangle! I feared he was being sucked into a vortex, but knew that on this occasion, I was the last person who could help him escape it. There was a reason our meetings were now fewer and it took a while until the identity of his new love was revealed, and the circumstances in which they had met.

13

The Showy Business of Beauty

DESPITE A FAIRLY hectic social life, I was more focused than ever on attempting to climb the greasy pole of journalism. Having by now discovered that writing arts features and dance reviews, or breaking into the BBC or commercial TV with new programme ideas, was a hard nut to crack, I refused to be cast down and simply waited to get a foot in the door of some other interesting sphere of journalism. It seemed that none of the obstacles I encountered in the field of arts coverage applied to other specialised areas of the press.

The beauty industry, for example, was undergoing rapid and radical changes. Whereas in the 1950s and 1960s articles on makeup, skin and hair-care were often tagged onto the fashion pages of newspapers, by the 1970s beauty had evolved into a high profile, consumer-driven market. At its core was a multi-million dollar global skin care and cosmetics industry: the accompanying marketing extravaganza with its product launches, scientific breakthroughs, fashion trends and tie-ins, as well as the boom in cosmetics advertising, joined the food, fashion, interiors and motor industries as a vital source of income for newspapers, magazines and television.

With the advent of good quality colour printing in magazines, and increasingly in newspapers, a new phenomenon emerged. The so-called 'special supplement', which included illustrated double-page beauty 'spreads', specialist magazines and pull-out feature 'sections', became integral to the success of commercial publications, especially where women made up a large percentage of the readership.

With advertisers and editorial departments vying with one another for more space to run ever splashier headlines, eye-grabbing photos and revelatory copy, there also arrived on the scene a new breed of specialised and authoritative journalist and editor – the Beauty Editor. Or, more prestigious still, the Health and Beauty Editor.

Health and beauty were merging. Until then, a vast chasm existed between the gossamer- soft-focus realms of makeup, hair styles and skincare on the one hand and, on the other, the scientific, evidence-based world of medicine. Advice on health and medical subjects were often written by professional doctors, generally male and middle-aged, earning a spare buck as part-time journalists for the popular press. In contrast, the subject of emotional and mental wellbeing remained a wasteland, occasionally and perfunctorily covered by the more progressive 'Agony Aunts' like Marjorie Proops, Clare Rayner and Anna Raeburn, as part of their advice on relationships, teenage sex, divorce and family problems.

Just as nature abhors a vacuum, so the gap between these two spheres was eventually filled by a new voice of expertise. The idea that one journalist should be simultaneously drawn to 'hard' and 'fluffy' subjects and write authoritatively on both, seemed, to many, unlikely and impossible. But, by the mid 1970s, one such all-round authority was creating seismic waves in women's magazines. Leslie Kenton, the daughter of American jazz musician Stan Kenton, seemed to arrive out of nowhere to become the Beauty and Health Editor of the upmarket monthly glossy, *Harper's and Queen*. By the time I began writing for *Vogue*, Lesley had attained diva status and had the beauty and health industries at her feet.

Tall, blonde and beautiful, with a permanent sun-kissed California glow – emphasised by her preference for wearing only white – she conveyed an artless image of natural beauty and inner wellbeing, unlike the high-varnished artifice of the cosmetics world. As she looked, so she wrote. Long, in-depth articles that leant heavily on scientific findings and cutting-edge research, each feature embedded with scientific studies and statistics from around the world. 'Fluffy' was an alien concept to Leslie and, whether writing about a new skin moisturiser, diet or slimming treatment, her approach was as acutely analytical – and as compellingly readable – as her reviews of new contraceptive methods, treatments for heart disease, stroke or stress-related illness.

Such was her sphere of influence over beauty and healthcare advertising that she was often given exclusive access to a new product before its official launch. While other journalists and editors were banned from writing about a new product, which remained embargoed until 'launch day', Leslie would often write a scintillating preview of the product. Inside information from the manufacturers – especially the giant corporations like Estée Lauder, Revlon and Lancome – including interviews with the laboratory staff and dermatologists who created the new products, was offered to her as an exclusive before the rest of the beauty pack.

I once overheard her at a product launch telling one of the directors of a nutrition supplements company that when *Harper's and Queen* first approached her to become their new beauty editor, she accepted only on condition that she could cover health and medical subjects to an equal extent. It was largely due to her success in pushing the boundaries in magazine publishing that a year or two later, no self-respecting 'beauty writer' would dream of limiting themselves to subjects that went only skin-deep.

Taking Leslie Kenton as a role model, and having stepped away from acting and show business, I thought about looking for a staff job on a magazine or newspaper. Harold thought it was an excellent way to establish a name and reputation, learn more about the publishing industry, and crucially, make more contacts in the business. However, very few journalistic or editors' jobs ever seemed to be advertised. I soon learned that journalists – especially beginners like me – did not use literary agents unless they also wrote books. Even then, an author's agent would almost never find or recommend journalistic work or staff jobs to their clients, since news of such vacancies almost always emerged via the gossip mill.

It therefore helped to know as many people as possible in the business: ambitious journalists who wanted to get ahead knew the importance of cultivating contacts among editors and commissioning staff. New editorial staff seemed to be chosen from within the trade: young, relatively inexperienced writers from provincial newspapers often applying to join national publications as assistants, or those with lowly jobs being gradually promoted within the ranks of a magazine or newspaper.

Occasionally, in the realm of upmarket women's magazines owned by the major publishing stables like Condé Nast, IPC, or the National Magazine Company – the UK division of the American Hearst publishing empire – an ambitious young staffer on, say, *Vogue,* might hear on the grapevine of a job going on a rival magazine, like *Cosmopolitan*, apply for the job and jump ship.

Otherwise, news of job vacancies came by word of mouth – sometimes via circuitous routes. When an actor and writer friend, Hedger Wallace, mentioned that a novelist friend of his knew a journalist with connections to the IPC publishing conglomerate – a part of the massive combined Daily Mirror Newspapers and Reed International organisation – and that there was a job going on one of the upmarket glossy magazines, at first

I didn't pay much attention. But Hedger called again to say this 'friend of a friend' knew the Features Editor of the upmarket glossy, and she confirmed they were looking for a new editor of one of the magazine's sections.

Now I took it more seriously.

"Are you interested in going up for the job?" asked Hedger.

"Perhaps… It depends for which section they need a new editor."

Hedger was none the wiser about whether the section was fashion, features, travel, entertainment, or anything else, but said he would try to find out. I thought no more about it until several weeks later he called back again.

"It's beauty. Apparently, everything to do with one's appearance. Also women's wellbeing and health."

Now he was talking!

"You're sure? That they're looking for a health and beauty editor?"

"Positive. Are you interested in going for an interview? The features editor can arrange it."

It was a no-brainer. The next day, I got a call from Betty Reyburn, the magazine's Canadian features editor, who set up a meeting for the following week. The name of the magazine, a well-known and popular title catering to young and early middle-aged women in the upper and middle income bracket, was *Woman's Journal.*

On a bleak January day, I set off for the offices of *Woman's Journal* in the IPC headquarters, a brutalist tower block in Stamford Street on the South Bank, just past the National Theatre and London Weekend TV Studios. The Editor-in-Chief, Laurie Purden, a stylish fifty-something *grande dame*, had an amused, quizzical manner that reminded me of the notoriously camp actress Coral Browne. Her number two, the editor Anne Gregg, blonde, pretty and outgoing, was beginning to make a name for herself covering foreign travel for BBC TV and was in the running to present its new holiday programme.

With merely a cursory glance at my cuttings portfolio, both women seemed more interested in how I saw the 'role' of beauty and health editor on the chic and aspirational *Woman's Journal*. Did I see health as a vital component of looks and beauty? How did I view the image and lifestyle of working women in the late 20th century? Was it possible to be good-looking without living a healthy life? Were budget cosmetics as effective as the global luxury brands? It was obvious that, as in TV or stage work, they were looking for a certain 'type' of editor, an image that reflected the upmarket 'brand' of the magazine.

Several days later, I had a letter from Anne Gregg offering me the job, followed by a phone call asking me to pop in to discuss the salary and arrange a starting date. With a working trip to New York already firmed up and articles commissioned by *Vogue* in the pipeline, we agreed I should begin working for *Woman's Journal* a few months later, in early June.

After that second meeting, I left the IPC offices and walked down the road to Waterloo in a trance. Landing a staff job as the editor of one of the most important sections on a leading magazine was the last thing I imagined would happen so soon into my new career. And of course I couldn't wait to tell Harold. His response arrived typewritten on *Daily Mail* notepaper.

> *Dearest Alix,*
>
> *This is a dictated note - but to put it on record. OFFICIALLY!*
>
> *I truly am delighted with the news you gave me the other evening. (I must watch it, however, as I am clearly in danger of becoming President of the Alix Fan Club!)*
>
> *But (a) you should feel most gratified at landing this appointment from an entirely self-taught start; (b) it is entirely a right decision because even if you don't stay there a lifetime (though it would be wise to give it a reasonable whirl), it does give you the status of being on the mast head;*

and, when other things come up, you will be surprised how valuable this is.

It is a shame (say I) we see too little of each other - but I hope that in the end you don't feel me guilty of unconcern in "what you are up to" - well, some of it!

Every success, I will keep you posted - but not boringly so on my problems - and please don't forget to give my warmest wishes to someone whom you know I hold in very high esteem: your mother.

Warmest regards, Harold.

* * *

News travels fast in publishing and before I had even signed my contract, I began receiving calls from different beauty PR departments and representatives of the health industry, inviting me to lunch, and even on foreign trips. And so it was that I accompanied my role model, Leslie Kenton, on a three-day trip to Paris with our host, the press lady for the vintage French skincare firm Orlane.

Because Leslie projected such an image of asceticism and clean living – she called herself a Buddhist and was one of the first people I met who meditated and fasted regularly, ate raw vegetables, nuts and grains accompanied by copious amounts of spring water and herbal tea – I dreaded the prospect of sharing lunches and dinners on our Paris trip.

There was no need to worry. We stayed in the Hotel George V and the Orlane PR lady took us to several of the finest Parisian haute cuisine restaurants including the then iconic Laperouse. There, I discovered that beneath the vegan hair shirt beat the heart of a shameless hedonist and *bon viveur*. She and I not only gorged on the finest faux-filet, Boeuf Wellington, escargots and cassoulet, but to my amazement she was also a connoisseur and lover of fine Bordeaux and Chateauneuf du Pape. Back home, she may have subsisted on nut cutlets and grated carrots washed down with Volvic, but off the leash abroad she clearly relished *La Grande Bouffe* as much as I did.

Following the Paris trip, I went to New York to research several *Vogue* articles. There, I discovered the sheer 'grandness' of some of the big American cosmetics corporations. This however was grandness verging on crass snobbery. When the London PR at Estée Lauder heard of my appointment to *Woman's Journal*, she arranged for me to meet her American counterpart in the firm's New York headquarters. Once there, and installed in a large, centrally located branch of the co-ed YMCA in Midtown Manhattan, I found the Lauder press office had laid on a presentation of their latest skincare collection by the Vice-President of Marketing.

In addition, they organised a trip to the company's laboratories in Long Island to meet their Research and Development team responsible for the manufacture and fine-tuning of products. Lastly, I was invited to interview the famous 'society' dermatologist, Dr Norman Orentreich, who had created the Clinique skincare range, one of Estée Lauder's most successful youth-oriented brands.

That visit to New York provided a crash course in the power and politics of major cosmetics empires. It didn't get more powerful than Estée Lauder Inc., at that time the world's last privately owned global cosmetics corporation. During my stay, the company showered me with gifts including flowers, chocolates and lavish presentation boxes of their newest skincare, makeup and perfumes.

But when they checked where in Manhattan they should deliver these packages, I discovered the ludicrous extent of the snobbery and elitism of the industry's top echelons. Hearing that I was staying at the YWCA, the press office refused to send anything there and requested that I arrange another delivery location, preferably with a doorman. What was probably embarrassing – and undoubtedly incomprehensible – to the

Lauder organisation, was to me hilarious. The idea that the Beauty and Health Editor of a leading British magazine – to which the organisation annually paid millions of dollars in advertising – should be slumming it in a youth hostel and not luxuriating in a swanky boutique hotel was, according to this elite powerhouse, nothing short of scandalous.

As I arranged for the packages to be delivered to a friend's East Side apartment, I realised that while I had quit theatre and TV as a performer, I was stepping into another world as image-obsessed and reliant on smoke and mirrors as show business. In fact, more so.

14

Going Legit

I WAS BARELY an hour into my new job at *Woman's Journal* when all the IPC journalists threatened to go on strike. Apparently, I was the cause and consequently it fell to me to avert industrial action, according to the Features Editor Betty Reyburn, who had helped me to get the job in the first place.

Marching into my office in a state of high agitation, she came straight to the point.

"You aren't a union member, are you?"

I shook my head. I had no idea which union she was talking about.

"You've got to join the National Union of Journalists right now, Alix! The rest of IPC is going on strike on the dot of midday unless you sign up this minute. Here's the NUJ subs' phone number – call them now."

I did not realise at the time that when she was juggling too many balls in the air, Betty could be vague and occasionally forgetful. In this case, what had slipped her mind was that she had phoned me before I took up my job at WJ, asking me to sign up to the Institute of Journalism, of which she was a member.

As a seasoned pro, she believed writers should support smaller select institutions over and above universally recognised organisations, a view I shared in principle. So I did as she requested. Not realising that, compared to the all-powerful National Union of Journalists, the IOJ was lesser known and relatively unimportant within the industry, therefore not recognised by all other trade unions.

By midday, I had become a *bona fide* NUJ member and a strike was averted. In other ways, too, my first day at the office was very different from what I expected. The small office was crammed with flowers, cards and bottles of champagne from well-wishers, mainly the various directors, press officers and marketing teams from every cosmetics and healthcare company in the UK as well as quite a few in the US and Europe. This showering of gifts and foliage was not dissimilar to a theatrical dressing room on first night. A large stack of letters lay on my desk: invitations to lunch, drinks, and 'working breakfasts' tumbled out, accompanied by press releases for upcoming and newly launched product ranges.

Several feet from my desk sat an exceptionally pretty, almost doll-like young woman at a smaller desk. Although I didn't know it then, Deborah Worth, a senior police superintendent's daughter and my new secretary and PA, would become my right-hand woman and partner in crime in many ways over the following years.

Spontaneously outgoing, charming and articulate, with an engaging chuckle, Deborah, aged just twenty-two, had mastered the art of multitasking, speedily bashing away at her typewriter while deciphering my impenetrable handwriting, updating our filing system and coolly handling endless phone calls. With a confident phone manner way beyond her years, she seemed to know instinctively which calls to transfer to my line, which to deal with herself, or whom to advise to call back later. Deborah and I almost instantly formed a relaxed, almost conspiratorial relationship, sharing laughs, gossip and business news to the point that she seemed more like a younger sister than my assistant.

As the days and weeks passed, nothing prepared me for how much time and energy was taken up with socialising, albeit masquerading as business. For the first month of my editorship, the phone rang incessantly with calls from the marketing and PR staff representing both leading and obscure cosmetics firms, hairdressers, perfumiers, health food and vitamin supplement manufacturers, pharmaceutical companies, gyms and exercise centres. All wanted to make an appointment to visit the office, or to invite me to lunch to "talk about the brand", "walk you through the method" or "introduce you to the range", while quizzing me about the themes, subjects and content of future issues of the magazine, the better to plan their company's forthcoming advertising.

Some invitations were hard to resist – being more a process of seduction than business, especially for a sybarite like me. I was lured into taking fitness classes and yoga lessons; invited to test gym equipment; spend hours luxuriating in new health clubs and spas while submitting to an array of facials, massages and other pampering. The old trope, 'tough work but someone has to do it', sprang to mind. I only had one worry: with so many hedonistic pursuits, when was there time to fit in all the real work, the research and writing?

It did not take long to realise that, unlike my former freelance status when my time was my own, I had to strictly ration my days and weeks, block out no go sections in my diary in order to meet all the commitments and duties that came with the territory. And, of course, make time to write – especially when up against uncomfortably tight deadlines.

The most important lesson I learnt was to steer clear of office politics, an especially disruptive element in an editorial team – and also the greatest time-waster. The only immoveable fixture was the fortnightly 'Editorial Meeting' held in Laurie Purden's office, where every editor and contributor crowded together for several hours to discuss new article ideas, pitch suggestions for future issues of WJ and discuss upcoming events and promotions. I was not alone in finding these meetings both overlong and physically uncomfortable. Not only was every member of staff encouraged to discuss their ideas at length, heads of other departments were obliged to sit and listen as cigarette smoke engulfed the room, leaving eyes stinging and mouths sticky with the fumes of stale nicotine.

Since everyone at WJ kept their office doors open, supposedly an invitation for colleagues to pop in and out at random for a chat, it wasn't easy to escape or remain indifferent to office gossip, feuds, vendettas or divisive policies. Thankfully, my office was in a cul-de-sac at the end of a long corridor, therefore the last of all the editors' offices. No passers-by could drift in for a chat en route elsewhere. It also helped that the sub-editors' office was opposite mine and, as I discovered, sub-editors are a breed apart, more preoccupied with fact-checking, layout and correcting journalists' grammar and spelling, so they tend to keep to themselves.

Best of all, two steps away from me was the magazine's large art department, an L-shaped studio occupying a vast outer corner of the seventh floor. The art director, Roger Hart, ran a tight ship, which was rarely disturbed except when Laurie Purden or Anne Gregg came to inspect contact sheets and photographic slides before choosing a cover for the next issue, or selecting illustrations for special features. With jazz or R&B music echoing moodily in the background, the art room was a world apart. Most of Roger's team, five or six young designers, graphic artists, photographers and general assistants, sat silently hunched over their desks, drawing boards and light boxes, peering intently at their work; some of the team were often out of the office on photo shoots, scouting for props and searching for locations.

Another secret I discovered was not to socialise too much with colleagues. While some staff shared lunch breaks or went for drinks after office hours, I preferred to spend my lunch hour alone, shopping or going for a walk after a quick sandwich – an IPC bus ferried staff from the offices via Waterloo Bridge to

Covent Garden and back again several times during that time of day. At the end of the afternoon, I was happy to get home as soon as possible, since I either had social events lined up or an article to finish and drinking in bars and pubs held no attraction for me. Thankfully, the commute was painless: a quick journey from Waterloo to Baker Street, and never was I more thankful for the temporary rush hour entrance to Baker Street station at the corner of Chiltern Street, several steps from my door.

In other ways, the quick commute proved even more of a boon when I began bending the rules of my work schedule. Once I found how much the noise and distraction at the office disrupted my concentration, especially when writing a particularly long, complex feature, I knew there was only one way for me to work more efficiently. When deadlines loomed, I signalled to Deborah that I was making an early exit from the office to work at home. Soon accustomed to my hybrid home-office work pattern, she held the fort brilliantly, diplomatically handling questions from my editors, the art department or the subs, phoning me if there were pending dramas and accurately predicting gathering storm clouds.

I don't know how soon Laurie Purden and Anne Gregg became aware of my '11th hour work from home' habit, but since they seemed happy with my work for the magazine, they never complained or questioned my work schedule. If they had, my response would have been what I always told Deborah. "If there's a problem or anyone needs me, I am only twenty minutes away on the Bakerloo."

On the domestic front, for once things were running smoothly. My cousin Sandy, a decade my junior, had been sharing the flat since beginning art college, where she studied architecture and interior design. She worked hard, had a quiet social life and usually stayed in her room as David Bowie or Pink Floyd drifted down the corridor. At other times, she sat by candlelight trying to work out problems and riddles with the help of the I-Ching or a deck of Tarot cards.

One of her passing boyfriends was Steve Harley, an East End journalist who wrote music and sang in his spare time. Sandy, who found Steve too old-fashioned and correct for her liking, eventually gave him his marching orders. A few years later, he went on to fame and fortune as leader of the band Cockney Rebel.

Once Sandy graduated from college, started her career and moved in with her boyfriend, whom she eventually married, I found two other flatmates who also led calm, harmonious lives. Granville Lee-Warner, a young, Greek-born actor, had attended a British public school and went on to study acting at the Webber Douglas Academy, one of London's leading drama schools. As with Helen Biden, my long-time flatmate, I also got to know Granville's Greek family, including his mother, aunt and sister and remained friendly with them long after Granville moved out.

Following in Granville's footsteps came Latvian-born Dace Remanez, who grew up in Canada before coming to London. By day, Dace lived a life of hermit-like simplicity, working part-time in the old Swan and Edgar department store in Piccadilly Circus. She had few possessions, a tiny wardrobe of clothes and liked to bake wholemeal bread twice a week, which she ate accompanied by cups of black coffee and little else, swearing the combination was more effective for the bowels than any constipation remedy.

At night, she worked as a croupier at Crockfords in Mayfair, which now catered mainly to wealthy businessmen from the oil-rich Arab states. Dace was a fund of inside information about this world of smoke and mirrors. I had only visited a casino a few times, and, lacking any appetite for gambling, found them boring, uncomfortably smoke-filled, claustrophobic places. When I joined a group of journalists on a lavish three-day press trip to Monte Carlo organised by Revlon, we stayed at the celebrated luxury Hotel de Paris, opposite the Casino and Régine's nightclub. One visit to that iconic yet underwhelming casino reinforced my jaded view of gambling.

Dace's stories bolstered my impression that even the smartest, most exclusive casinos, far from being glamorous, were in fact elite salons for the largely desperate and self-deluded, frequented by big-stakes clients with shady backgrounds and money to burn. Many of the 'punters' she encountered were 'professional' gamblers, or hardened gambling addicts, mistakenly convinced they had perfected a 'system' to break the bank.

However, gambling provided Dace with the opportunity to realise her ambitions. By putting aside a large part of her weekly salary and lavish tips, she eventually saved enough to return to Canada and start her own real estate business.

At a time when a new chapter had begun in my working life, this long period of unusual domestic harmony was a welcome change. My time was taken up with hard work, getting to grips with editorial duties, which included work-related social events and foreign travel – these were the days of lavish press junkets, often in luxurious foreign locations, in the name of 'research'. There was no question of turning down these invitations, since each one of us editors was expected to attend as an ambassador for our respective magazines.

Across the landing, Harold's life seemed more than usually complicated, in part because the new woman in his life had turned his usual peripatetic existence into an even greater spin. Despite lapses in our face-to-face meetings, his letters and cards were still a most uplifting mix of the surreal and the droll, told in abbreviated capsule language with a liberal sprinkling of lists and bullet points.

Darling Alix

From: The Ayatollah of N.U.PE.

Alas (and sorry)... I have no fresh milk; only 'Carnation', which isn't bad with coffee (it's outside your door).

Will be interested to hear more, very interested, on your last excursion.

*Had a most extraordinary few days myself – more ways than one *see below. But one in particular; ie. gave lunch* <u>*on successive days*</u> *(yes!) to the following :*

Angela Neustatter - "THE GUARDIAN"

Jean Dobson - "THE SUN"

Ann Boyd - "THE OBSERVER"

Lesley Ebetts - "THE MIRROR"

Jane Proctor - "COUNTRY LIFE"

And A. N. Other

I don't want you please to repeat this - but F A S C I N A T I N G - I mean a kind of CATWALK MAFIA in one brisk gallop!

I have a mental block. I put an idea to Gerald [Gerald Rudge, editor of Femail]. *He wrote back to me suggesting: "Ideal for Alix Kirsta". Did I put his note in your mail box?*

There is a 'suggestion' I go to prison on Thursday. But wait! I do have a choice. Nonetheless I have never been to prison and new experiences diminish as "the days dwindle down to a precious few". My doctor would urge the prison hospital: a total rest. This is serious. But I guess I chicken out in the end... then despise myself for cowardice.

Love, H

As the weeks passed, I learned that the new object of Harold's affections was married –apparently happily and to an extremely nice man. German-born Gisela Hendy and her English husband, Vernon, owned a bookshop around the corner from Harold's Brighton flat, which is where she first met him when he wandered in looking for a book about bread. They got chatting – the attraction was instant and mutual. But I never discovered any more than that – even when I eventually met Gisela in Harold's flat, a warm, bright and outgoing young woman with a soft accent, delightful sense of humour, and great knowledge of art and literature. Judging by some of Harold's letters, however, there were turbulent periods before he and Gisela settled into a permanent relationship.

Dearest Alix, (which I mean!)

How can I possibly extricate myself from this bondage of bad behaviour which I've put myself into?

Dreadful, dreadful, dreadful!

First, obviously my warmest thanx for the magnificent bottle I found outside my door. (I shall NOT DRINK the contents... though I feel only some alcoholic oblivion can blot out the really bad feelings I have about messages left unanswered. There is a limit; I desperately hope I haven't this time overstepped it.

Oh yes, there are explanations. A year now (and though professionally I'm told "functioning well"!), still no real answer to what I am suffering from. [Numerous medical tests for recurring stomach problems had not yielded a diagnosis, though I knew he feared it might be cancer.]

Mary's sister's husband seems terminally ill [Harold's sister-in-law Pat, with whom he remained close, was the younger sister of his first wife, Mary, killed in the car crash in which both were involved in 1959] *and I've been anxious to help there. Middlesex Hospital.*

Behaving – even within the wretched parameters of my (laughingly-called) private life – with complications – complicated complications – also.

Strikes. The entire "Mail" produced for four days by the editorial people: not fifty or fifteen, FIVE. During this time I was living 'near the shop', at the Savoy – hence the 'no-lights' situation. The other 'no-lights' occasion (see paragraph starred green above, about my private life) I was living near Bath at a place with the ridiculous telephone exchange of Compton Dildo.

And so it goes.

You're probably tonight watching Liza Minelli at Covent Garden but I shall ring.

And thank you.

And have you seen the current issue of "Confectioner, Tobacconist and Newsagent"? No? You should!

Love

Harold

Even though Britain had endured a long period of national humiliation, bedevilled by the sobriquet 'The Sick Man of Europe', by 1979 the worst miseries of the decade seemed slowly to be coming to an end. These included galloping inflation, low industrial productivity, the global oil crisis, a national coal strike, the three-day week and wave after crippling wave of illegal wildcat strikes accompanied by violent picketing, demonstrations and protests. The aptly-named 'Winter of Discontent', when countless public service workers including rubbish collectors and grave diggers went on strike, finally eased off in spring 1979. Among the weary public was a sense of relief that the Seventies were drawing to a close, with fresh hope that a newly elected Tory government, led by Margaret Thatcher, would restore growth and prosperity.

For me, cocooned in the fragrant world of women's magazines rather than mucking in down the road in the sweary bear pit of Fleet Street, it was tempting and too easy to become detached from all this everyday ugliness. An odd mix of compassion fatigue and imperviousness to violence and terror muddied the minds and wore down the spirits of many Brits during the latter part of the decade. Relentless graphic TV coverage of bloodshed and barbarity had lost its power to shock, perhaps because much of the UK had by now learned to live with the widely publicised horror of frequent IRA bombings in our major cities.

Further afield, escalating sectarian violence, terrorism and state-sanctioned carnage were the stuff of nightly TV news: and with so many atrocities playing out night after night on our screens, from the Iranian Islamic revolution to the civil wars in Nicaragua and Chile, anxiety and despondency became my automatic responses.

It often took a few lines from Harold to put all the sleaze and horror into perspective –perhaps because of his way with a cryptic aside and the characteristically droll irony with which he summed up the bloodshed and mayhem.

As when I wrote a note asking him whether he had seen a particularly grotesque, cold-blooded assassination covered live on TV. Bill Stewart, a 37-year-old American ABC TV news reporter, was on assignment in Nicaragua when his clearly marked press vehicle was stopped in Managua by government soldiers from the country's civil guard. Despite having the word *Press* emblazoned on his flak jacket, he was forced out of the van, ordered to kneel, then lie face down on the ground where he was kicked by several guards, one of whom then shot him through the ear, killing him instantly. The sickening slaughter was filmed from inside the van by Stewart's cameraman: the live footage went out several hours later around the world.

Dearest Alix,

I'm sorry you're feeling "downish" – that makes two of us "caught up in the gale of the world".

It's 2am and I just have your generous note.

Yes, I did see the whimsical murder of the TV reporter. Incredible! But then the mad old wanker, Khomeini, isn't doing too badly in the Department of Death, is he?

Do you know the Ayatollah of Portman Mansions? He worries me too. [This was a Saudi businessman living in a flat across the road from our block, whom I had seen standing at the French windows for long periods in his white robe, rubbing his groin as he gazed absent-mindedly at the street below.]

Did you know (few people do) that Mr J. Thorpe (onetime Liberal leader) has spent the last two nights in a prison cell, for the first time? His bail automatically cancelled – and one request from that spooky judge – that this fact must not be* *reported, means just that! No paper, no TV news programme dare ignore His Lordship's simple: "I suggest to you that it may be better if you don't", etc... etc...*

** the first 'media' judge*

PS. Did you read him saying, "The kind of man who has a cocktail cabinet in his sitting room". Of course! But is it relevant? [During the sensational six-week trial of former Liberal leader Jeremy Thorpe and three other men for conspiracy to murder Thorpe's lover Norman Scott, Thorpe and his co-defendants had been free on bail. As customary under British criminal law, bail was withdrawn once the case went to the jury. After deliberating for six hours without reaching a verdict, the jury retired to a hotel, and Thorpe remained in custody in Brixton. Two days later, Thorpe and his co-defendants were acquitted on all charges.]

I don't require the magazines, outside, returned.

And let's try again. Let's!

Love

H

As always, Harold continued to be perplexed and outraged by some of the more irritating small print of life around him, and that included Portman Mansions. Having railed for years against our management company's failure to maintain the dilapidated lift, despite what he called its "ritual smashing up" by four Libyan children living two floors below, his attention now focused on an unfortunate middle-aged couple living in the flat beneath him.

The couple, who at first glance appeared dull and colourless, could have stepped out of Edward Albee's *Who's Afraid of Virginia Woolf?* Their rows played out, as if on cue, at weekends or bank holidays, starting in the morning and petering out before lunchtime. Because I lived on the opposite side of their back windows, I could only hear occasional words and phrases floating up from below. Beginning with low-level sniping, accusations and recriminations, this was a well-rehearsed ritual, a set-piece which built to a crescendo of profanities until the mutual disembowelment was complete. Followed by a deafening silence.

Harold on the other hand, because he lived directly above, received the full impact of the blast. To his irritation, the disturbances were becoming more frequent.

Dearest Alix,

I turn now to the explosions in the flat below: they are becoming a cause for concern.

"Whit" Sunday provided a lively assassination of love: well, OK, that was a Sunday.

But Whit Monday was a lulu: well, understandable perhaps as a public holiday.

But this morning is neither a state or a religious day of celebration, and has truly kept me awake since 6.30. One wonders if perhaps they use electronic amplification of any kind, as these old flats are normally well sound-proofed. I never get the radiogram or that insane laughter of TV audiences which many flats suffer from.

Today however, amid the obscenities and blasphemies, clear lines came floating upward: "I have one wish, just ONE WISH – to slit your fucking throat from ear to ear."

Is it a case for the Marriage Guidance Council? I have 'friends' there who certainly succeeded in 'guiding' two marriages I know over the brink of total calamity.

Is it a matter for the police – in the sense of 'committing a public nuisance' or 'disturbing the peace'?

Whatever – it now goes far beyond the acceptable limits of a normal Sunday morning punch-up.

Pray advise me.

Love, H

* * *

As the months passed, I became busier and busier. One reason was that every year, *Woman's Journal* held one or two important 'readers' events' in which all the editors, including Laurie Purden and Anne Gregg, were prominently involved. The main fixture was the annual *Woman's Journal* Readers' Day at the Savoy Hotel. Always popular and oversubscribed, it provided a varied and entertaining occasion for two hundred readers to meet the names behind big fashion, beauty, health and food brands, and chat to the editors. It was a well-organised hybrid event combining elements of entertainment, sales promotion and marketing, talks and advice, all wrapped up in a day's luxury and socialising.

It was a long day, beginning with morning coffee, followed by upbeat promotional entertainment; in my first year, this was a short dance demonstration incorporating simple keep-fit exercises by London's Dance Centre. Then came a fashion show featuring new collections from Jaeger, Max Mara and others, and a buffet lunch. We editors worked the room, mixing and mingling, answering readers' questions, giving a few minutes' talk and introducing the next 'celebrity' fashion or make-up expert.

With the likes of Estée Lauder representatives, astrologer Patric Walker and society milliner David Shilling taking part, it was also a camp, high profile occasion. The only disaster, from my point of view, was that my friend Bernard 'BJ' Hall, let me down massively – though few in the audience suspected anything had gone wrong. Bernard, then teaching keep-fit classes at the Dance Centre studios in Covent Garden, had been booked to kick off the morning with a ten-minute exercise session featuring himself and six Dance Centre students.

At 11.15, a quarter of an hour before he was scheduled to give the demonstration, Bernard staggered into the Savoy's River Room, unsteady on his feet, with an ominously glazed expression. He had obviously been on a massive bender and forgotten why he was there or what he was supposed to do.

"You have only ten minutes before the number," I hissed in his ear. "Get changed in the gent's – the girls are waiting to go on."

He stared at me, terror in his eyes.

"Darling, I can't. I'm ill, my legs have gone. I can't see properly. Forgive me, you'll have to get someone else to go on."

Thankfully, one of the girls waiting to do the routine was Carol Hayes, the Dance Centre's dynamic publicity officer. Standing nearby, she saw BJ's condition and my horrified expression, put two and two together and stepped in.

"Don't worry, BJ, you're not well. I'll front the number, I know the exercises."

Minutes later, she and the other girls ran onto the podium and launched into a fast, high energy routine, their motivational whoops and yells accompanying the pounding disco beat. The event was a success, but it was almost a year before I talked to Bernard again.

Despite my full-time job, I did not want to lose out on freelance work for other publications. Not only did I enjoy the variety, I also thought it important to maintain contacts with other publications and commissioning editors. I knew that other magazine employees managed to juggle staff and freelance work, so when I was commissioned by *The Daily Mail,* as well as *The Daily Express,* to contribute articles, I asked Laurie Purden for permission. She agreed but asked me to use another name. Which is how the byline Alexandra Cruickshank – the surname was my stepfather's – began to appear. When the Publicity Manager of Marks & Spencer's publishing department approached me to write a beauty book for their stores, I accepted provided I could use the pseudonym.

A year into the *Woman's Journal* job, other opportunities drifted onto the horizon. Harold, who was a close friend and former colleague of Deirdre McSharry, the editor of *Cosmopolitan,* mentioned that the magazine's high-profile Beauty Editor, Pattie Barron, had been headhunted by the New York *Daily News* and there might be a vacancy for her job on *Cosmopolitan*. He realised that I might not want to leave *Woman's Journal* quite so early in my editorship, but asked me if I would like him to have a word with McSharry about arranging an informal meeting. I agreed it might be a good idea, but when her office called to make an appointment, I eventually had to cancel the date at short notice because of a crisis at the office.

> *Darling Alix,*
>
> *Now why do you do it? Why do you make appointments with editors – nice editors, efficient editors, but sometimes prickly and edgy editors... and then chuck the appointment? Why?*
>
> *I ring Deirdre to tell her what a great girl you are, what untapped talent and so on – and this is what I'm told!*
>
> *You can't imagine what a switch it is to be writing a letter like this to someone else instead of sinning exactly the same way myself...*
>
> *But folly it is! Whether you are the sinner or I am.*
>
> *Goodness me, though, I'm delighted with the news of your "Vogue" successes. You know I'm not fooling, I really am.* [Two of my Vogue articles had been published belatedly, though in fairly rapid succession, well after I joined Woman's Journal.]
>
> *Herewith the letters you asked for, and thanx for letting me see them.*
>
> *As we never do meet (or very seldom), I'd better sign myself...*
>
> *CO-POSTPONER or PUTTER-OFFER...*

My meeting with Deirdre McSharry was rescheduled several months later. Apart from the occasional foray to *Vogue's* offices in Hanover Square, a haven of hushed corridors and low-key elegance, this was my first visit to the offices of another magazine. By comparison, the National Magazine Company, off Carnaby Street, teemed with chatter and the non-stop coming and going of delivery drivers, couriers, models, photographers and the staff of about a dozen different magazines including *Good Housekeeping, Elle, Country Living, Esquire, Cosmopolitan and Harper's & Queen*.

Visiting *Cosmopolitan* was also my first experience of open-plan offices, and I was taken aback to see even the editor-in-chief sitting in the middle of a large and busy room, with only two temporary half-screens either side of her desk to mark out her plot from those of other editors and journalists.

Even though I was by then used to meeting editors whom I had never worked for, I found McSharry daunting. Although she came across as surprisingly casual, even laid-back, there was a slight *froideur* – or was it simply quintessential British reserve, a quality which, coming from a continental background, I always found disconcerting especially in women? Although I had not come for a job interview, because Pattie Barron had recently departed for New York, the implication was that a vacancy might be in the offing.

I assumed that was why Deirdre McSharry spent some time explaining the magazine's ethos. Compared to *Woman's Journal*, its target readership was composed of young, single career women; the magazine's style, which had proved an unqualified success, was uniquely iconoclastic, sex- and youth-oriented and no subject was too risqué or intimate to be off-limits. She believed the best way of sustaining the magazine's freshness was through teamwork and close collaboration between all editors and staff. As she saw it, an open-plan office was the best environment in which to nurture such collaborative efforts.

When I asked her how her writers coped under extreme pressure and when they needed some quiet and privacy, she was clear.

"If things get very pressured before a deadline or going to press, there is a small room down the hall where someone can go off to write for an hour or two. They don't leave the office. No one goes home to work. We don't want people going off and working in an ivory tower."

I think both McSharry and I realised that the all-muck-in mentality and collegiate style at *Cosmopolitan* – very different from anything I had come across in the field but undeniably effective under McSharry's leadership – was too inflexible and unforgiving of individuality for my temperament. Eventually, I did work a lot for The National Magazine Company, but it was as a freelance writer and never for *Cosmopolitan*.

Again, Harold's response to my thoughts on meeting McSharry was forceful and unequivocal.

Dearest Alix,

Even by your excellent standards this is a very funny note.

Nor are your judgments wildly awry. Our friend can be a seemingly sleepy lioness – and one sudden clout of her paw and your face is ripped open. And even your references to 'toffee' and saucers of milk I at least do understand.

But my relationship with the lady has been a strange one (professional; and I'm very fond of her and I know she's bloody good: what she says I always find worth listening to.

Just let me add this. Her comments about you were absolutely gratuitous: I hadn't even brought up the name before she did (though I did say one or two things later which may be helpful).

I'll tell you more.

Don't undervalue Miss Deirdre McS! Actually I'll be seeing her again, I think, before the week is out. H

15

Moving On

ALTHOUGH DEIRDRE MCSHARRY and I did not meet again, my job on *WJ* – as Harold forecast when I first accepted their offer – continued to generate more contacts and opportunities. Some came to fruition; others did not. Barbara Timms, my commissioning editor on *Vogue*, called to invite me to lunch with the editor-in-chief of British *Vogue*, the formidable Beatrix Miller. Although Felicity Clark, the respected *doyenne* of beauty writing, was *Vogue's* long-established Beauty Editor, Beatrix Miller thought it was time the magazine appointed a Health and Fitness Editor. Furthermore, as Barbara informed me on the phone: "I have told Beatrix Miller, Alix Kirsta is who you should have in the post."

Both flattered and excited, I joined them for lunch and was relieved to find Beatrix Miller less imperious than I anticipated. She immediately came to the point and told me I would be right for the job – but acknowledged that it would be neither honourable nor professional for me to resign from *Woman's Journal* right then, less than a year after starting the job.

"I think you should remain in your present position for a while longer and when the time is right, we can offer you a contract at Condé Nast."

Reassured that she understood my predicament and was prepared to wait for me to join *Vogue,* we parted in agreement. After almost six months, just as I began to consider resigning from *Woman's Journal* in order to move to *Vogue*, I picked up the latest copy of the magazine and saw a new name, Deborah Hutton, on the masthead as Health and Fitness Editor. Perhaps for the first time I doubted whether being principled and doing the 'right thing' was always wise when it came to a career move. As for trusting an editor's words, even when the editor was someone as iconic as Beatrix Miller, I had learnt my lesson.

More successful was a phone call out of the blue from a literary agent, Felicity Bryan, who was with one of the UK's leading agencies, Curtis Brown. She wanted to meet me, having just read one of my articles in *Woman's Journal* called *Sex Is Good For You*. Less raunchy than its title, the feature looked at the beneficial physical and psychological side effects of falling in love, sexual attraction and a regular sex life. Over lunch, Felicity said the subject was commercial and provocative enough to make a good book, and would I be interested in joining the agency? I readily accepted, while confessing I had little time at that moment to write a book of such length and complexity, but emphasising that I definitely planned to write books in the future.

Felicity Bryan was happy to leave the issue of a future 'sex book' open and sent me a contract. At last, I had a literary agent – one of the best.

I was seeing less and less of Harold as time progressed, and our conversations on the phone were fewer. What concerned me was that his letters – now more infrequent – were darker, underscored by anxiety and with more than the usual quota of gallows humour. Knowing he spent much of his time with Gisela, I was thankful that he was rarely at home alone and could count on her unwavering care and support, especially when unwell.

Dearest Alix,

(From an exhausted, harassed and overworked Gisela, I gather you now know of my maddening predicament.)

Why didn't I tell you?

It's true that ours is a friendship which will ride heavy weather. Alas, it's also true that the fairly crazy irresponsible 'programming' of my life often leads me to neglect matters which shouldn't be neglected – for example keeping in touch with you, as I'd actually like to.

But one thing I cannot tolerate and will never be guilty of, namely: ONLY communicating when the game is running badly for you and "Help!" is the cry to be heard in the hills. Hence I feel it inappropriate to parade my very real misfortunes, which date right back to a certain fatal car crash 20 years ago (Query: has my life ever been under control, read control, since? End Query.)

I'm bound to say, though, I never ceased to regard you as a 'loyalist' in true emergency, however little deserved. Presumptuous? Say "No".

So now I feel free to get in touch and will: because I'd certainly like to hear your news – you know that – and here I am under house arrest, with extra elements of what David [David English, Editor of the Daily Mail] *calls "Keeble's capacity for Chaos" thrown in. Yeah... me? I'm in a mess!*

I hope all prospers. Are you around this weekend? (Heard that before?) I AM. (Really I AM, scout's honour).

Harold... with love.

PS: Lennon. [John Lennon had just been murdered outside his Manhattan apartment.] *What a day for a newspaper junkie to be imprisoned! In its subtleties, the story has everything, a mystique imposed on it out of proportion to the event itself. Thirty seconds of mindless violence which encapsulates the whole idiocy of our times*

His periods of enforced bed rest – usually on doctor's orders – became more frequent. Apart from chronic heart problem sometimes accompanied by fatigue, I gathered from Gisela that Harold continued to suffer severe abdominal pain, while undergoing countless scans and tests to establish the cause. He seemed by now convinced that he had cancer, and was understandably frightened at the prospect. On the odd occasion when I did see him in the hall, he looked frail, having lost weight and failed to top up his customary Brighton suntan.

Dearest Alix,

No one is trying to 'frisk' or 'quiz' you, kid, but am I right in thinking: NO lights in your place early in the week? Been away?

Alas, your Friendly Neighbour's Medical Bulletin is pretty sombre. My transition 1980/81 has been terrible - AND IS.

Positively don't want to go on and on - but 'nut-shelled', the situation is that this long-standing intestinal trouble now really is back with new intensity and frequency. All the time, in fact.

I confess to dismay because I've had long remission periods - the bloody thing has been active for two years, remember - and there seemed some good hope that it was clearing itself, which it could.

[NOTE: Oh God, yes - further boring news - at least my back trouble did vanish more or less on schedule?]

But this! New dimensions altogether!

To sum up...

Buky's self-appointed stand-in - maybe understandably - just didn't function: to be blunt, he was locked into the problems of securing that practice. [Harold's doctor, Dr Buky, had died suddenly of a heart attack, leaving a colleague in temporary charge of the practice.]

So! New doctor – Lionel's – in whom I do have faith. But the appalling reality of all those records – I'm talking not of hundreds but thousands of pounds – simply 'not there'... well, it means a fresh start on all tests, this time via the Middlesex and the new doctor. [When Harold changed doctors, all his medical records were lost.]

Agreed, this is probably inevitable as the present deterioration puts a whole new face on everything.

I'm sure, Alix, I can count on you to keep this to yourself as they tell me "it's a small world", isn't it? Answer: "YES, ours is... so please..."

I should know more Tuesday – but for once I am, finally, despondent. The two-home, professional/emotional aspects – oh everything ! – is so difficult when you're crocked and immobilised. But, whatever the news is, I'd like to keep it private to handle my way. You understand, I guess.

Gisela has problems, too! She's coming up late tonight, however and through tomorrow we'll be trying to sort out a 'game-plan'.

I've good reason to think you do care so I won't hesitate to keep you updated. Indeed, in this also unfortunate Queenie situation [his housekeeper had been diagnosed with cancer and undergone chemotherapy so could only work part-time], *she's doing nobly, marvellously, but it's not the answer, is it? Another problem.*

Tough truth, as I've always said, is: LIFE GOOD, provided one isn't stricken with something which isn't trivial; for then my lifestyle (HA!) can so quickly crash.

Alix, I have your statue to return [a bronze which Tom Merrifield, the former dancer turned sculptor had created of me]*... tomorrow may be a bit 'crowded', as next major session, Middlesex, 1 am Monday. One's instincts say I shall be 'beckoned' which, though it may superficially seem to solve a domestic problem possibly, IS NOT 'good news'.*

In hospital, I mean.

Real disappointment is – I had seemed to be phasing out of major trouble here and also the whole medical cock-up scenario is a sickener.

Put no money on me for the next Olympics!

Sorry long letter but I did want you to know: your mother (to whom my best) likewise.

Love H

The updates on his health left me with a heavy heart. Even after years of communicating frankly about his health problems, I knew his condition was becoming increasingly serious and he was more despondent than I had ever known him to be. Familiar elements of chaos, as with his lost medical records, which were once amusing, now only added to his burden.

While the drama played out silently next door, and down in Brighton, I was having one of my most hectic years, professionally and socially. I was able to share some of those events with Harold on the phone or by letter, and he continued to quiz me about my news, in large part because it amused him and momentarily took his mind off his troubles. His distractions were few, since he spent more time working at home, often editing and designing layouts from bed, than at the office.

Several of what he called my 'escapades' especially entertained him. As when I arranged with Laurie Purden to interview Estée Lauder, the *grande dame* herself, on one of her visits to London for the UK rollout of a new make-up range. The interview was arranged by a new PR at Lauder's UK headquarters, Lyn Leigh, who invited me to the New Grosvenor Street offices for an exclusive meeting with Mrs Lauder.

Lauder was friendly and outgoing, happy to answer my questions about her Hungarian connections and early life in New York where she began creating homemade skin creams and eventually launched her company.

Unfortunately, she then decided it was time to demonstrate her central 'philosophy' of beauty – the importance of a 'glow' in achieving a beautiful complexion. Looking at my largely makeup-free face – my daily 'look' had always been minimal, outdoorsy, with only mascara and a dab of nude lipstick – she said, "I'll show you." Before I could escape, she ham-fistedly set about daubing my face with the company's new product range, applying foundation, fluffing on powder and, despite my protestations, stippling my cheeks with a sickly shade of pink blusher, lips topped off with a vile slash of magenta lipstick.

"There – *now* you've got a glow!" enthused Mrs Lauder, ignoring my scowl and obvious discomfort. "Every woman's gotta have a glow – that's what lights up the room," she cooed, brandishing a mirror triumphantly in front of me to reveal her handiwork. A clown with a bad makeup job stared back. In the background, Lyn Leigh, clearly reluctant to step in, wore a pained expression, and muttered to her boss, "Pretty. Very pretty, Mrs Lauder."

Back in the office, I told Laurie Purden that the interview had gone awry, I had little material and could not write up the piece.

Not missing a beat, Laurie responded, "Impossible. The interview stays. We must run the piece. Lauder have bought two extra double page advertising spreads for that issue."

In the end, Laurie and I managed to cobble together an 800-word 'puff piece' about Mrs Lauder and everyone was happy. And I learnt a valuable lesson in the economics of glossy publications. On the positive side, the incident led to Lyn Leigh and I becoming close friends, even after she moved to New York to become vice-president of public relations for Aramis, the Lauder corporation's top men's range.

Other stories that made Harold chuckle included my interviewing Elaine Stritch on her beauty secrets. Still resident at the Savoy, she was starring in a TV series with Donald Sinden and by then I had met her several times socially, and she was relaxed about sharing her thoughts and tips. These were surprisingly puritanical, especially about the use of cosmetic surgery to look younger. "Never! Make the most of what nature gave you. Trying to cheat age is far too risky. My motto has always been: don't fuck around with God!"

Harold was especially keen to hear about my foreign press trips. The highlights included an invitation to Berlin from the German pharmaceutical company Schering, one of the leading manufacturers of the contraceptive pill. Our group consisted largely of medical journalists, with only a couple of non-science writers like myself. This was my favourite type of press event, since it involved learning about a specific area of medicine through in-depth lectures with ample opportunity to question Schering's medical team.

Although we stayed in a first class hotel near West Berlin's Kurfurstendamm, the real eye-opener was an organised bus tour of East Berlin, crossing Checkpoint Charlie with an East German guide smugly extolling the virtues of the Eastern Bloc over the inequities of Western capitalism. It was a dismal and sobering afternoon. The city and its neglected buildings, the dimly-lit streets, queues of shabby residents outside down-at-heel groceries with their sad offerings of shrivelled fruit and vegetables, was as grimly devoid of grace notes as I had always imagined Soviet Bloc countries to be.

Another 'educational' press trip, which turned out to be unintentionally amusing, was a trip to Brussels arranged by Van Den Bergh, manufacturers of Flora low-fat sunflower spread. The theme of the trip, again attended chiefly by science journalists, was the link between diet and cardiovascular health, and how the contrasting epidemiology of the two separate parts of Belgium, the French-speaking and the Flemish regions, was linked to the different types of diet popular in each area.

The event kicked off with serious lectures about the ill-effects of a typical high-fat French diet of meat, cream, sauces, full-fat cheese and butter, compared to the low fat Flemish alternatives. Next came an organised tour of several supermarkets which catered principally to Flemish residents, statistically healthier and less likely to suffer heart disease. These stocked an abundant choice of clearly labelled, low-fat alternatives; healthy yoghurts, skimmed milk and olive oil, or Flora-style polyunsaturated vegetable spreads.

But the unexpected surprise for us journalists came at lunch and dinner. Brussels being one of Europe's great centres of gastronomy, for two days the directors of Van Den Bergh, including a team of nutritionists and medical researchers, joined us in gastronomic blow-outs consisting of the finest classic rich French cuisine and wines. The early Eighties had not yet encountered *Nouvelle Cuisine* or *Cuisine Minceur*, which subsequently shook up French restaurants. Had it taken place a year or two later, the deliciously ironic Flora press trip would have looked very different.

Back at IPC, the horizon was beginning to shift. Late in 1981, I had a call from Penny Radford, a former editor of *Woman*, one of IPC's oldest women's weeklies, whom I had met some years earlier when she interviewed me for the post of Assistant Beauty Editor. She was about to start work on a new glossy women's monthly, currently in the planning stages and scheduled to hit the stands the following year. Would I like to meet to discuss being the Health and Beauty Editor?

Over two years had passed since I joined *Woman's Journal,* and I was considering moving on sometime the following year. I was beginning to feel constrained by the formulaic nature of the work, and by the very real limits on extra mural activities such as writing books or freelancing for different newspapers and magazines. The new magazine sounded interesting, so I agreed to meet Penny, its new editor, to find out more.

I wanted to ask Harold what he thought about my moving to another publication but, not having heard from him for several weeks, I avoided bothering him in case his health had taken a turn for the worse. When I heard from Gisela that he had gone into hospital for an indeterminate period, I jumped to dire conclusions. But, a week later, a letter arrived which allayed my – and of course his – worst fears.

Darling Alix,

To update you.

I got back yesterday from seven days in a public ward in the Middlesex.

And with good news on the Big Issue – but all is not yet Cheers Unlimited.

It was an experience that retrospectively – indeed, as enacted – I won't easily forget: with more cynical friends saying: "Typical! When you read everywhere about the Private Medicine Boom, he has to go NHS!" Though I hadn't actually got either a card or a number!

No question that when I went in, the expectation was very major surgery as the x-rays seemed to be cancer-positive.

Slightly complicated story, won't burden you with it now, but as of the present... ***NO****. No cancer.*

I do believe that without question I've been in the hands of the man considered probably the No. 1 on gastro-intestinal matters. The attention lavished on me – some of it highly uncomfortable – was quite beyond belief. But daunting. At one point there seemed even to be a throat connection and – yes, I did meet Jack Hawkins after the operation...

When there's time (very soon I hope), I'll give you the picture as compactly as possible. I got back yesterday – and I truly am exhausted; but obviously up-cheered also.

Gisela has been marvellous – somehow she got up every day but at what price (not money, I don't mean) to her!

A final touch of farce in my exit. The moment 'The Great Man' cleared me, they wanted that bed next morning! OUT!

Queenie, poor Queenie, is quite ill – and she had one set of keys. Gisela, at 10 am, was in Brighton with the other set.

And Queenie had taken all my clothes.

I left the Middlesex (in an office car) in silk pyjamas a) expecting to be arrested; b) yesterday was a very nippy day – freezing point – to be at the porter's lodge (to collect a spare set of keys) Chiltern Street in thin pyjamas and even thinner robe.

Me and The NHS... ah well! H

PS. This calls for no reply, Alix, truly. I thought you'd want to know however. Indeed, I much wanted you to visit me in the Madame Alice Letitia Axton bed. King George V Ward. Bed 9. It's high on the list of Beds I Have Known. H

So I see on Ceefax...

It's Official

Murdoch has got it! Have you seen "The Eye" this week? [Rupert Murdoch, who already owned *The Sun* and the *News of the World*, had made a controversial bid to buy *The Times* and *The Sunday Times*. Despite alarm among the Labour Party that he was in danger of dominating the UK Media, Margaret Thatcher's government waved the bid through, neglecting to first refer Murdoch to the Monopolies and Mergers Commission. On 22nd January 1981, Murdoch took over Times Newspapers.]

When we finally had time to talk, Harold elaborated on the numbers of exploratory procedures he had been forced to undergo – some of which he didn't know even existed. These included endoscopies and colonoscopies, which provided a live tour of the highways and byways of his digestive system, from oesophagus to bowels. The final verdict was that he was not suffering from cancer. Harold's relief at the diagnosis was almost eclipsed by his enthusiasm over how new technology was transforming medicine.

His diagnosis, after all, was possible only because of a recent medical revolution: the development of fibre optics and computer technology which was beginning to offer a window onto the interior of the human body. Doctors could now carry out precise and forensic detective work by inserting a thin, flexible tube fitted with a light and miniature camera capable of filming every nook, cranny and square millimetre of the gut in close-up. More crucially, by transmitting these images to a computer screen, every abnormality of the digestive system could be meticulously analysed and diagnosed. Which is how Harold's team found that the cause of the searing pain he had suffered for almost two years was caused by a large and active gastric ulcer.

Unfortunately, that was only half the story. Diagnosis was one thing: treatment another. In the early 1980s, doctors believed – incorrectly, as it emerged – that ulcers were the by-product of extreme stress and over-rich, spicy food. There was no cure for ulcers, and standard treatment consisted of a bland diet, antacid medication and a more relaxed lifestyle. Only in rare cases was surgery recommended to partially remove the stomach.

Given Harold's chronic cardiovascular problems, his medical team decided it would be too risky to subject him to major abdominal surgery and decided instead to try and manage the ulcer with medication and a change of diet. He was, of course, the last possible candidate for a less stressful lifestyle. It was not until the late 1980s, with the discovery that the majority of stomach ulcers are caused by a bacterial infection called Helicobacter-Pylori, curable with a course of antibiotics, that the treatment of ulcers was revolutionised.

So Harold's problems were far from over. The pain and fatigue caused by his ulcer came and went, periods of remission were followed by severe attacks out of the blue. The condition –coupled with his chronic heart problems – meant he was forced to take it easy over the following weeks: as he grew stronger, he returned to the office while continuing also to work on and off from home, whether in Portman Mansions or Brighton, with Gisela by his side.

As a result I saw little of him. By the end of the year, I decided to accept Penny Radford's offer to become Health and Beauty

Editor of *Options*, which had all the makings of a refreshingly modern women's monthly, and was to launch in spring 1982. I started planning ahead and decided I would leave *Woman's Journal* three years after starting my job there. During that final year, there was much work to get on with: Laurie had decided to launch a special 'stand-alone' health and beauty supplement under my editorship and, because I contributed only a couple of long articles to the supplement, I had to commission other writers to contribute features and later rewrite many of these if they failed to come up to scratch.

One of the year's highlights that Harold especially enjoyed hearing about was my visit to Hong Kong, which in every way lived up to his previous thrilling description as a unique place, crackling with energy, every bit as high-octane and pulsating with enterprise and commerce as New York. Ironically, I went as a tourist, not on magazine business, since my boyfriend, a New Zealand photographer with whom I was now living, was commissioned to photograph a variety of spreads for *Woman's Journal*.

Less inspiring was a press trip to Tangier at the start of winter, for the launch of a new range of sunscreen products. We journalists were joined by a photographer and a couple of models booked for a Moroccan beach photo shoot under sunny skies for the company's upcoming advertising campaign. Obviously no one had consulted the meteorological office to check the weather in North Africa in December. We touched down in misty, rain-lashed Tangier and after a freezing night at the hotel, immediately headed for the nearest *souk* to buy umbrellas, woolly shawls and jackets. For three wet, windy and miserably cold days, we hunkered down in the hotel, lingered over extended lunches and dinners, trudged through deep mud to see an outdoor local market, tried to stay warm sipping scalding sugary tea in smoke-filled Moroccan bars as the rain continued hammering down. With no let-up in the weather, the photo shoot was cancelled and rescheduled for the following March in Gambia. I returned with a streaming cold, aching joints and muscle pain in my legs and arms.

Around New Year, Harold was planning to resume some of his social activities and ease himself back into a more hands-on structured work schedule. Life was looking up and he sounded cheerier and more upbeat than he had been for a very long time.

Dearest Alix,

Formal thanx for your welcome and most interesting note with its glimpse - merely a glimpse - of fascinating frontiers of NEWS!

Listen! Why don't we make a real, genuine, 18-carat effort to have dinner/lunch? (Telephone me now if you're awake and it's convenient - or in the morning otherwise - that is, if you'd like to.)

I have a few days 'fixed up', but not many - so let's arrange it and keep to it, even if it's ten days or so from now.

I can also scatter possibly the odd news item here and there - and not about the bloody bathroom! Disregard that! Though I mustn't disregard its consequences, [there had been a leak in his bathroom, damaging the ceiling of the flat below, and he was having trouble getting the managing agents to organise repairs] *honestly it's been terrible and no Queenie for ten days until today - but it's recovering.*

I won't disturb you tonight but give me a call - here or at 353 1761 - whenever you wish.

We have grim newspaper problems (others likewise), but my day was brightened by hearing a girl, apparently very inadequate in bed, described as "Lay Miserable".

As ever

Harold

On a bitterly cold day in early March, we met for lunch at one of his – and my – favourite restaurants, the White Tower, a fashionable Greek restaurant in Fitzrovia. He ordered his usual roast duck, which, as he always explained, was uniquely crispy because the chef removed the fat before cooking, roasting the skin separately from the bird. "Isn't that clever?" he enthused. "It means there's very little fattiness in the meat but you get this wonderful crisp skin."

True to form, he was eager to hear my news. I was looking forward to my first trip to the Caribbean. *Woman's Journal's* art director, Roger Hart and my photographer boyfriend Ken Martin, had arranged with the Jamaican Tourist Association for Air Jamaica to provide free flights and hotel rooms on the island in return for a lavishly illustrated Summer Beauty supplement, shot entirely on location at various idyllic spots.

Harold was noticeably thinner, making me feel instinctively protective. His shirt collar no longer fitted snugly around his neck, the once round face was drawn and tired, and he had what he dismissed as "the beginnings" of a cough.

"It's nothing serious, a bit of a cold. I'm taking a couple of days off tomorrow to get rid of it."

Otherwise, he was in cracking form, mentally focused, energised by the week's breaking news, speculating about current scandals, and asking which of the latest West End shows were worth booking. I updated him on *Options*, the new magazine being launched the following month and which I was joining that summer after completing my three-year tenure at *Woman's Journal*. Reassuringly, he agreed it was time for me to move on and branch out as a writer and not waste time and energy on office politics. This was especially true in my case, since I had no ambition to become an editor; all I wanted was to write and take on the challenge of a greater range of subjects.

Time flew, and all too soon he had to return to the *Daily Mail*. As I walked him to a waiting company car, he kissed my cheek and wished me a safe and interesting trip. He had been to

Jamaica several times, to visit his friend Ian Fleming when the *Daily Express* serialised the first James Bond novels in the 1950s, and was struck by the island's spectacular beauty – as well as its crime rate. "Be careful. Watch your step. Call me when you're back and tell me your news," he said with a grin, as the chauffeur held the door open for him.

The Jamaican trip lasted longer than originally planned. Over dinner with two friends –Lyn Leigh, the PR from Estée Lauder and another girlfriend who was planning to get away on holiday – I suggested it would be fun if they both joined me in Jamaica after the *Woman's Journal* shoot. Cheap air fares were available since the peak winter holiday season in the Caribbean was ending, and I was able to book us all a discount at one of the leading hotels in the smart resort of Ochos Rios.

It was a memorable trip. Prime photo locations included palm-fringed beaches; powdery pink sand offset by turquoise sea and cloudless cerulean skies. A tourist representative led us to idyllic, off-the-beat tropical rainforests, waterfalls, caves inhabited by serried ranks of bats hanging upside-down as if on a washing line. To 'dress' the photo shoots, we had our pick of every existing tropical fruit, giant flowers and foliage, as exotic birds sashayed around, flaunting their technicolour plumage. The photos were spectacular, a perfect blend of exotic and classy.

When Roger, Ken and our model returned to London after nine days, I decamped from the low-key chic Sans Soucis Hotel in Ochos Rios to another sumptuous, Colonial-style hotel nearby, where the tourist office had managed to arrange a special rate for us.

After ten days of swimming, sunbathing, hiking, sightseeing, jet-skiing and pampered indolence, the three of us arrived back at Heathrow in the early morning of April 5th to leaden skies, cold and rain. The adventure was over. As Lyn and Sophie waited for our suitcases by the baggage carousel, I headed to a vacant public phone to let my mother know I had arrived home safely.

"Hello, darling, what good timing. Your flight seems to be on time. Did you have a wonderful time?"

But before I could say more than a few words, she cut in, her tone serious. "Look, there's something I have to tell you."

"Is everything alright at home? You're not ill, are you?"

Quickly she cut in again.

"I'm afraid it's bad news. It's Harold."

A boulder hit my stomach.

"What's happened?"

"A heart attack. A few days ago. Harold is dead."

16

Rummaging and Resurrection

IT WAS A miserable homecoming. By the time our taxi dropped Lyn, Sophie and me at our respective homes, I had stopped crying; what remained was a crushing sadness. Back at Portman Mansions, I dreaded taking the lift to the top floor, where the first thing that met my eye were dozens of black rubbish bags outside Harold's door and a few more piled alongside the trash bins on the emergency fire exit.

Harold's door was slightly ajar; inside, the hall was dark and silent, though obviously someone was inside in charge of the clearout. But who? Queenie? Gisela? The porter or the managing agents? For a second, I thought of calling out, but felt too miserable to chat to anyone. I picked up a large, framed black and white photograph that was poking out from one of the garbage bags. Eight men in dinner jackets seated at a formal restaurant table. The caption read: *Daily Mail Dinner at the Savoy Hotel 1948.* Among the diners was the film producer Alexander Korda, broadcasting mogul Lord Bernstein and Harold, slightly in profile, elegant, handsome, with a slight smile. A lump arose in my throat. I slid the picture into my bag and unlocked my front door.

Harold had died in the early hours of 31st March and the funeral had already taken place. A few days later, the memorial service at St Bride's, the 'journalists' church' in Fleet Street, was packed. Five minutes into the service, a man in a pew a few rows ahead of me started to sob, his shoulders shaking. It was Bob Edwards, former editor of the *Daily Mirror* and several other newspapers, who had worked with Harold before he went to the new-look *Daily Mail.* I had known Bob long before I even dipped a toe into journalism, after he blatantly chatted me up on a train as it pulled into Maidenhead Station, me visiting my mother at the farm, he en route home to his wife and children.

I was then twenty-one, still in show business, and Bob stylishly wined and dined me several times before making a surreptitious gentlemanly proposition one evening. It was a pass so tentatively low-key that I had no trouble graciously rejecting him without causing either of us embarrassment. Bob's evident grief over Harold's death surprised me, since I had never once heard Harold mention his former colleague. Since I assumed Bob must have been deeply fond of Harold, I wanted to talk to him after the service but he left before I could approach him.

Instead, I stopped to talk to Queenie, and then Gisela, who seemed to me to be still in shock, given her surprising poise and good humour as she welcomed mourners. Promising to tell me later about the circumstances of Harold's death, she added that he had phoned her the evening after he and I had last met for lunch.

"He told me 'I've just had lunch with a tree!'", referring to the new 'dangling leaf' suede jacket I wore a lot at that time. "He thought your jacket was amazing, so original. It really made an impression on him."

Later, I found out more about Harold's last few weeks and days. The 'minor' cough and cold he had dismissed when we lunched the previous month was no such thing. By early March, he became gravely ill with flu and was unable to work or get out of bed. He stayed at Portman Mansions as his temperature soared; although taking only codeine, he began to hallucinate. One evening, he phoned Gisela who heard him becoming confused, telling her that the two decorative cockerels opposite his bed were attacking him. Terrified, he smashed them against the bedroom wall.

Only at that late stage, on a Saturday night, did his doctor send over a prescription for antibiotics while Gisela dashed up from Brighton and trawled London after midnight in search of a twenty-four-hour chemist to get the medicine. She looked after him in London, then in Brighton, until he became stronger and his old friend Lionel Green invited him to stay at his Mayfair home while he recuperated fully.

Away from his domestic woes, which included delayed structural repairs in his Brighton flat and problems arising with his lease, he thrived in the luxury and comfort of Lionel's home, grateful for the cosseting lavished on him by Lionel, his wife Judy and their housekeeper. Within a fortnight he made good progress; Lionel encouraged him to have visitors over for drinks and tea, until, at the end of March, he felt strong enough to go back into *The Daily Mail.*

"He had a profitable day at the office," Gisela remembered. "Later in the evening, he joined Lionel and some friends for dinner at a restaurant. Afterwards, he phoned me for a debriefing and was in a highly excited state about being back at work and had greatly enjoyed the company that evening."

On their return to Upper Grosvenor Street and after Harold's call to Gisela, Lionel and Harold chatted for a bit and then went to bed. The following morning when the housekeeper came to wake Harold, she found him motionless in bed, still clutching his latest toy, a Walkman cassette player on which he had been listening to music.

A post-mortem gave the cause of death as a major coronary thrombosis. I consoled myself with the thought that he had probably died in his sleep, not in fear or pain or after a long, lingering illness. Gisela reminded me that when his doctor, Buky, had died unexpectedly some years previously, doing what he loved best, going to bed early and listening to classical music, Harold remarked, "That's how the lucky ones go." His wish to die like Buky was fulfilled. But far too soon.

Belatedly, I managed to read several obituaries saved for me by a close friend who had met Harold at Portman Mansions when she lived there with me in the 1960s. There were fulsome tributes. *The Times* hailed him as '*an éminence grise extraordinaire… who was a star as a young man bursting upon national newspapers* and *a star when he died yesterday… Some of the great names of Fleet Street admit that without him they would have never made a mark.*'

The most celebrated of these great names was his old friend since the 1950s, Lord Snowdon: '*He will be appallingly missed by people like myself – not only as a good friend, but as the man who, quite literally, invented photo-journalism. It is not that our pictures were good in those days at the Daily Express; it was the way that he laid them out in the paper that made them great.*'

Harold's last newspaper, *The Daily Mail*, headlined the death of the legendary 'Wizard of Fleet Street' with a subtitle so punchy he might have written it himself. '[He] *who put a touch of magic into your life six days in every week.*' Both the paper's owner, Lord Rothermere, and its editor, David English, remarked on his extraordinarily active forty-six year career, during which, said Rothermere, '*he never grew old.*' He was lauded as '*one of the great figures in the history of Fleet Street who through his unparalleled career as a senior editor managed to remain on top for longer than any of his contemporaries*'.

As David English commented: '*His impact on British journalism can be seen in every newspaper published today. He was always – right up to the last minute – the freshest and most youthful of journalists. He had more friends in the profession than any other journalist of his time.*'

Although I saw Gisela again briefly several years later, when I visited her and Vernon's bookshop in Brighton, I later heard she and Vernon had sold the shop and she and I lost touch.

What I did not know at the time was that Harold's death in 1982 and the gap it left in my life, was the first of a series of seismic tremors that turned my world upside down. Having resigned from *Woman's Journal*, much to Laurie Purden's displeasure – "Penny Radford should know better than to go poaching other magazines' staff, she knows it isn't done" – I started work at *Options* early that autumn, only to find that Penny, who had edited the launch issue of the magazine, had been replaced as editor by Sally O'Sullivan, whom I did not know.

It was agreed I would work largely from home, but I was also given half a desk in someone else's department at the *Options* offices in Newman Street, off Oxford Street. I contributed health and beauty articles for three issues and found Sally O'Sullivan perfectly civil, but lacking warmth or humour. Or professional *savoire faire*, as it eventually turned out.

At the end of the year, I picked up an advance issue of the magazine and chanced on a feature about acupuncture written by someone I had never heard of. The feature lit a touch paper. By that stage, I knew I had made a mistake jumping ship. It was a bad career move and, though I saw little point in staying on at *Options*, the blatant intrusion by a freelancer into my territory was beyond insulting. Or, as I told Sally O'Sullivan when I went to see her: "It's like a slap in the face with a wet fish." Thankfully, before I could resign as I planned, she suggested it might be better if we parted company – to which I readily agreed.

It was good to be freelance again. Having begun to write features for other magazines such as *Over 21*, *Harper's & Queen, New Woman, Working Woman* and *The Daily Mail*, I was also getting commissions again from *Vogue*, ironically from their new Health Editor, Deborah Hutton, who had taken the job *Vogue's* editor-in-chief had offered me two years earlier and with whom I got on well.

Around that time, I also came up with a book idea about the diverse ways in which human skin reflects our inner health and mental state. My agent sold the proposal to a relatively new publisher, Century, which was under the leadership of the brilliant Gail Rebuck, a trailblazer who soon became the most powerful figure in publishing.

Not long after I signed the contract with Century, my mother fell ill and after some months of mysterious and distressing symptoms, originally put down to depression, she was diagnosed with an inoperable brain tumour. As an only child, with my aunt living in Vienna and my cousin Sandy married and working in Florida, my friends became my sole source of care and support. Because my mother had been given only three months to live, I told Gail Rebuck I could not immediately start work on the book and she reassured me it wouldn't be a problem. So, within a few weeks of my mother's death shortly before Christmas 1983, I immersed myself in the long process of researching and writing the book, while living in New York for prolonged periods throughout 1984, which I regarded as a preliminary step to moving there for good.

It was a year of grieving, loneliness, feeling unanchored, while at the same time being immersed in hard work and confronted by tough and unfamiliar challenges. Apart from writing my first book, this included dealing with my mother's estate, selling her home and the farm, and searching for a new flat for myself. Because my mother, like Harold, was the 'protected' tenant at Portman Mansions, and therefore entitled to a fair rent, I was given notice to move out because those favourable terms did not extend to me. By summer 1985, while still planning to live in New York, I met the man with whom I soon settled down and eventually married; shortly afterwards, I bought my own flat, different in every way from Portman Mansions, in another part of London.

What eventually struck me was that I had done a lot of growing up. Not that I had much choice in the matter. In the midst of grieving for my mother, as well as saying goodbye to a young person's carefree way of life, now firmly in the past,

I found myself having to deal with the responsibilities and commitments placed on my shoulders without cracking up. Two major anchors – my mother and Harold – were gone, but far from caving in I felt strong, capable of making choices and taking decisions about work, finances and domestic life without either of my two rocks for support.

Reflecting on the previous fifteen years, I finally understood how the heartaches, challenges, career changes, the setbacks as well as the achievements, had bashed me into shape and made me stronger. And Harold had played a crucial role in making that happen.

One August day in 1985, I packed my bags, put away my memories, said goodbye to Portman Mansions and shut the door on a long chapter, before moving to my new home and a fresh beginning with the wise, funny, kind and brilliant lawyer with whom I had chosen to share my life.

* * *

2021

Our home was in need of a massive clearout. More boxes were stored in the attic than I ever imagined and the job of decluttering was long overdue. It also resulted, as these things inevitably do, in a trip down memory lane. Old press cuttings, show business photographs and publicity material, theatre programmes and cast lists of shows I had been in, my first journalism portfolios and tapes of TV and radio programmes in which I had taken part. Most went into the bin. Next came random boxes of letters, tied with blue velvet ribbon by my mother a long time ago; they were from my parents and grandparents and other relatives and went back to my early childhood: carefully, I laid them aside. Others from school friends, ex-boyfriends and aspiring boyfriends, I relegated to a recycling bag.

The last box I came to was extremely large, overstuffed and tightly bound with string to prevent the contents spilling from underneath the fragile, buckled lid. As I untied the string, the lid popped off, disgorging cards, envelopes and letters onto the floor. In a nanosecond, a kaleidoscope of yellow, red, green and brown notepaper and cards fanned out around me, their bold, multi-coloured messages as urgently assertive as the day they were written.

Words danced off the pages, decorated with bullet points, asterisks, lists, bold, in-your-face sub-headings in giant capitals, demanding attention.

> *Marriage before the year is out? Has the recent heat deranged your brain?;*
>
> *Remember, the only reason for marriage is when life without him is unthinkable;*
>
> *Come on now, cheer up. With a firm stride into the future;*
>
> *I realise this is none of my business but I think you are making a massive mistake;*
>
> *How about we meet at our usual hour, about 9.15 and head Savoy-ward for supper?*

As I skim-read them randomly, each letter fast-tracked me back to my twenties and early thirties, flashing up heart-stoppingly familiar images. The impact was both uncanny and shocking. Had my twenty-something self really been so totally idiotic and ridiculously immature? Why did I shed so many tears over those unavailable or unsuitable men? And how had I ever found the courage and confidence to turn my back on one precarious career and step blindly into another – similarly precarious for different reasons – about which I knew nothing?

After almost forty years, Harold was alive again and his impact on my life became dazzlingly clear. Quite simply, not only did I owe him my career but also the introduction to a life of endless opportunity, new challenges and unfamiliar paths, which inspired so many of the investigative features and books I went on to write after his death. The word 'mentor' seems too modest and bland to describe his role in shaping my future, as he nudged me onto the nursery slopes of journalism and guided me with encouragement and generosity of spirit whenever the going got tough. Far more than a mentor, he was a beloved friend, father figure and trusted confidant packed into one.

While the discovery of his letters brought Harold to life and the force of his personality shone as brightly now as in my youth, I was dismayed at how many questions about him remained unanswered. Harold rarely dated his letters and trying to fit his correspondence into the time-frame of our relationship was a frustrating and tricky business. Once I decided to flesh out the bones of the younger Harold Keeble, I had no inkling how difficult the task would be. Hours of trawling Google got me nowhere and old-style research didn't lead much further, either. Scouring newspaper archives and libraries yielded mere titbits, leaving me with a ragged, half-completed jigsaw with too many missing pieces.

It was only when I discovered books written by some of Harold's former Fleet Street colleagues that a troubling, somewhat alien picture began to emerge. What I read disturbed me deeply. In Bob Edwards' autobiography, *Goodbye To Fleet Street*, published in 1988 only a few years after Harold's death, he described Harold with a staggering mixture of spite and reverence as '*our resident genius… one of the greatest talents I have known*', while on the same page vilifying him as '*... utterly malevolent… his incurable treacherousness… nobody has ever handled pictures better… he was a star who had the unnerving habit of disappearing at moments of decision*'.

And this from the usually mild mannered editor I last saw sobbing at Harold's memorial service!

Another of Bob and Harold's colleagues, Mike Molloy, conjured up a similar Jekyll and Hyde image in his 2016 memoir, *The Happy Hack*. Acknowledging him as a Fleet Street 'legend', Molloy's book revealed that within the complex politics of the *Daily Mirror's* production department, a chasm existed between staff who '*liked or loathed Keeble*'.

Molloy described that when he was first shown the ropes as a rookie journalist on the paper, a long-time *Mirror* staffer told him that the night editor loathed the features department, where Molloy was hired to work. The alleged reason was that at the time, Harold was largely in charge of features and the night editor hated him. And apparently not just the night editor. "Everybody hates Keeble, except me, so now they all hate me too," confided the staffer.

Side-swipes abounded in similar vein. Molloy learned that the newspaper's staff photographers disliked Keeble, too, because of his habit of buying large quantities of freelance pictures, although one of the *Mirror's* art editors confessed that he and Keeble in fact liked one another. But once more, the story had a sting in the tail: the art editor explained to Molloy that when Harold arrived at the paper, he acted contemptuously towards all the staff until the art editor created some pages Harold had designed. "He liked the job I did, so I became his chosen boy. So now they all hate me, too."

Asking what Keeble's title was on the *Mirror*, Molloy discovered that he resolutely declined any formal position on the grounds that: "If you haven't got a title, no one is in charge of you. When he sees a part of the paper he wants to redesign, he just goes ahead and does it."

As I discovered, it got uglier. My queasiness over these savagings intensified when I was shown part of an early memoir by the gossip columnist Nigel Dempster, in which he reminisced about his days on the *Daily Express*. Given Dempster's *metier*, the deft sliding of a knife between a target's ribs was to be expected. However, since the memoir was published before 1982, Harold witnessed the treachery at first hand. In the galley proof I was shown, he had even scribbled his own disparaging comments in the margins.

Likening Harold to '*an amiable plump cherub who had by a quirk of fate survived into adult life*', Dempster recalled him as shrewd, ruthless and very ambitious. '*I learned to watch the smile and accompanying chuckle with care and some anxiety... behind the warm cherubic smile I sensed a* froideur *that would resist the warmth of a human relationship.*'

Like all Harold's detractors, Dempster could also gush: '*He was for a time in a class of his own… he used headlines, photographs and text with a bravado that made Fleet Street gasp with envy… he brought magazine-style design to daily papers and improved on it with dazzling artistry…*'

Further on, in another section that drips venom, Dempster insinuates that Harold had a hand in getting him sacked from the *Daily Express* by bad-mouthing him to the newspaper's proprietor, Lord Beaverbrook. But as Harold makes clear in the margin, Dempster is skating on thin ice given the potentially defamatory nature of the remarks. Whether the comments were cut from the final published book remains unclear, since no copies remain.

Who was this nasty piece of work, both revered and reviled? He certainly bore no resemblance to the man I knew. Unfortunately, by that stage it was almost impossible to speak to anyone Harold had worked with since most were now dead. Worst of all, when trying to reconnect with Gisela I drew a blank. The new owner of Kemptown Books, who had bought the shop from Vernon and Gisela, told me that they no longer lived in Brighton and he had no idea of their present whereabouts. An internet search produced no entries for the Hendys. I despaired of ever finding out who had inherited Harold's estate or acted as his executor. There was no clue to who owned the copyright of any books, articles and other written material. And, knowing he had no children and was himself an only child, it wasn't surprising that when I entered his name on two ancestry websites, I hit a dead end.

Eighteen months after rediscovering the letters, I made one last attempt to find Gisela, even though the previous trail had gone cold. Maybe she was dead, seriously ill or had returned to Germany – a possibility, especially since Brexit. Again, I typed her name into Google, without any mention of her husband Vernon or the name of their bookshop. This time, other German Christian names came up alongside the surname Hendy. Clicking on the entry, the link revealed someone listed on the residents' committee of a block of flats in Eastbourne.

There, I found that the Mrs Hendy in question was German, aged 74 and one of her middle names was Gisela: she had recently stepped down as company secretary of the residents' committee. Praying that she hadn't moved since, I dashed off a letter to her Eastbourne address. Thirty-six hours later, an email pinged into my in-box. It was from Gisela. Bloody-mindedness had paid off!

As flesh attached to the bones, I was even more appalled at how little I knew about Harold. He had made Gisela his sole heir and executor and her own laser-sharp recall allowed her to winkle out even the smallest obscure nuggets of his life in the decades before they met in 1978.

Far from having no relatives, she put me in touch with her old friend, Harold's sister-in-law Pat Buchanan, now 95 and living in a flat in Folkestone, her mind still active, her memories vibrant. Pat was overjoyed to be able to talk to me about Harold, whom she adored. She was the younger sister of Harold's first wife Mary, who died in the 1959 car crash in which he was injured, and her memories of her sister and Harold's love match emerged in sparkling detail.

It was a fairy story of glamour and romance. In 1945, immediately after the end of the war, which Mary had spent in the WRENS stationed at Dover Castle, she heard the *Daily Express* was holding a competition to find a young servicewoman who had worn uniform throughout the war, and was now about to be demobbed and return to Civvy Street. The winner would be given a makeover by the paper's experts, including revamped makeup and hairstyle as well as fashionable new outfits for a return to normal life.

"Mary dashed up to London from Dover at the last minute, unkempt and still in uniform. She had only read about the competition by chance that morning when she turned up at the *Daily Express* offices. Being tall, slim and beautiful, she was chosen for the series by various editors, the couturier Norman Hartnell and fashion illustrator Robb. They sent her to hairdressers, makeup artists, fashion experts and photographers and the transformations ran as a series of features in the paper."

Andrew Robb was a star contributor at the *Daily Express*, whose drawings illustrated the fashion pages. "He was gay, he and Mary hit it off and became great friends. He introduced her to Harold and the two fell madly in love, got engaged and were married in January 1947." Pat remembered it as a heady time, with her family swept up in a whirl of glamour and high living, being put up by Harold at the Savoy Hotel, where since the 1930s he remained a welcome habitué.

The wedding was a classy event; the service at the King's Chapel of the Savoy was followed by a glittering reception at the Savoy. Because Pat and Mary's father had died during the war, Mary was given away by the legendary *Daily Express* editor, Harold's boss, Arthur Christiansen. With the handsome and elegant Robb acting as Harold's best man, this was a stylish Fleet Street affair.

After a honeymoon in Paris and the French Alps, Mary and Harold moved into a spacious flat in Wigmore Street, next door to the recital venue, Wigmore Hall.

"It was very big and all white telephones, extremely smart. I saw my first TV in that flat. Later, they moved to Portman Mansions, another beautiful home where I often stayed with them."

What saddened me was how much tragedy devastated all their lives not long after those golden days. After Mary was killed in the 1959 car crash, their mother, who was widowed during the war, eventually committed suicide. Then Pat's first marriage ended.

"I got married far too young, to the wrong person, and of course it didn't work out," she told me.

Harold's second, seat-of-the-pants marriage to Susan Jacobs ended after less than two bumpy years, during which he suffered a coronary thrombosis and another protracted hospital stay.

Pat's second marriage, to the big love of her life, ended after twenty-five years when her husband died of cancer at the age of fifty. Much later, she also lost her daughter to breast cancer.

Another chilling revelation was that Harold, who was then the Associate Editor of the *Daily Express*, had been involved not only in one major road accident, the one in 1959 which killed Mary and his chauffeur, but another as well. Pat explained the full horror of what happened later.

"He spent six months in traction in St John and St Elizabeth Hospital in St John's Wood after surviving the crash in the first half of April. When he was discharged from hospital on 8th September, a Tuesday, he was still on crutches and went to his parents' home on the south coast to recuperate and begin working again. That weekend, Sunday 13th, his chauffeur-driven company car was involved in another accident near Caterham."

The September crash was more serious than the first, involving a three-vehicle pile-up, including a motorcycle, leaving two men dead and eleven seriously injured including Harold, who sustained extensive head injuries and severe shock.

A local ambulance took him to the nearest hospital in Caterham, and Pat recalled that he immediately phoned St John and St Elizabeth Hospital in London to get transferred. His response was characteristic. "He had only been out of there five days and said to them: 'Hold that bed. I'm coming back'. So back he went for another period of recovery. But this time he came out of hospital an alcoholic."

Letters of sympathy from colleagues and friends including Tony Armstrong-Jones, later Lord Snowdon – a frequent hospital visitor – and Harold's boss Lord Beaverbrook, reflect the affection in which he was held by his friends. Pat, however, believed there were too many others who, possibly unaware of the extent of his drink problem, visited the hospital bearing champagne and fine wines to cheer him up. But while this appalling second body blow, so soon after the previous sickening tragedy, knocked him sideways, increasing his need for oblivion, it seems unlikely that it led him to drink. That demon had come calling many years earlier.

According to Gisela, Harold claimed he did not start drinking until his mid-thirties, towards the end of the war. Pat, always close to Harold, confirmed a story that had long circulated in Fleet Street about Harold's office fridge, allegedly kept well stocked with Puilly Fuissé; by his desk stood an oxygen cylinder and mask in case he needed to sober up fast. The wine-stocked fridge and oxygen supply was an office fixture since the days when his colleague and fellow drinker, Sefton Delmer, longtime *Daily Express* correspondent and Harold's editor from the 'black propaganda' wartime years, shared his office at the newspaper.

It was hardly surprising, given Mary's death – especially the violent manner in which she was killed and Harold's attempt to drag her dead body from the car – coupled with his own extensive injuries, that physical pain and hospital confinement should drive him to drink far more than usual. And so it continued until, finally, the writing was on the wall. Following a coronary thrombosis, Harold's doctor delivered a final ultimatum: drink or die. As he often told me, giving up alcohol was the hardest battle of his life and once on the wagon, he never again touched a drink. Except once. Returning from abroad one evening, in a buoyant mood after an enjoyable holiday with a girlfriend, he went into the drawing room, opened a bottle of wine and knocked it back in one go. Mortified, and worse, unaware of any cause for the relapse, he phoned his doctor who arranged for him to dry out.

Harold was not the first member of his family to have a troubled relationship with alcohol. As I found out more about Harold's background, I learned that his maternal grandparents were part-owners, with another partner, of a paper mill outside

Dewsbury, and his uncle, his mother's brother, was given a job in the company. Some years later, when his uncle was found to have defrauded the business, the two partners worked out a deal to hush up the scandal: the young man would not be reported to the police, but, in return, Harold's grandfather, an alderman and highly respected pillar of the community, agreed to hand his share of the business to his partner. The good name of the family proved more important than justice and the integrity of the business.

Harold's disgraced uncle, who turned out to be an alcoholic, was banished to the United States where he married and started a family. What became of him remains a mystery. After Harold's death, Gisela was contacted by the uncle's daughter – Harold's niece – who was trying to trace her father, who abandoned their family when she was a child. Gisela heard no more from her since, leaving the whereabouts of Harold's niece unknown.

It also seems possible, even likely, that alcohol, albeit indirectly, played a part in one of Harold's more reckless acts of bravado – which he couldn't guess would bring devastating consequences.

Although I always assumed Harold had a congenital heart disorder, atrial fibrillation, which in later years was seriously aggravated by alcoholism, the truth I learnt from Gisela was more bizarre. In early middle-age and sound health, Harold entered a bet that he could swim in the sea from below his flat in Brighton to the pier. He won his bet. But at a hefty price. It left him on permanent medication for a fibrillating heart.

The man I was finally getting to know more fully was an infinitely more complex, troubled human being than I remembered from my youth. Only by learning more about him did I finally decipher the clues to his personality and recognise the darker forces that could cloud his usually positive, upbeat nature. It was all there in the writing, I only had to connect the dots. Once I re-read his letters, so many nuances and shifting moods emerged; clearly, I was too flighty and self-preoccupied to notice such subtleties the first time round.

After the sour taste that lingered from reading his detractors' cheap jibes, I was heartened to discover how many more people, people of consequence and character, loved and respected him. A letter to Harold from Lord Snowdon, not a man given to fulsome praise and hyperbole, revealed how much he – as well as the world of newspapers and photographers – owed his old friend and mentor.

> *My dear Harold,*
>
> *Your telegram meant more to me than I can express to you. Apart from being my personal patron since the early Fifties, always giving me wise encouragement, spontaneous responses and constructive criticism. You, and you alone, have done more to promote and use photography in the right way in newspapers, not only in this country but the world over.*
>
> *It was you who started showing fashion photographs outside of Vogue and therefore making the public at large more fashion conscious. Rightly appreciating the work of that much underrated John French, who started that whole era of bounced light which the television and film world is only just looking into thirty years later.*
>
> *It was you who influenced an entire new look with theatre and ballet photography by allowing the likes of us to use the small camera and capture the mood rather than worrying about the technical boring details... Before you came on the scene, photographers never even had a credit.*
>
> *And thank you also for always being a wonderful friend.*

In a letter to Harold's sister-in-law, Pat, the legendary hard-nosed columnist Jean Rook, better known for blistering attacks than heartfelt tributes, remembered her former editor as '*one of the greatest journalists of our time, and a man from whom I am proud to have learned very much about my profession while I was working for him*'.

Harold's name also featured prominently in a valedictory book about Fleet Street published in 1988, a time when the newspaper industry was in the process of abandoning its centuries' old domain, with newspaper offices decamping to such disparate neighbourhoods as Canary Wharf, Blackfriars, King's Cross and Kensington.

The book's contributors included dozens of journalists, editors, publishers and artists, each reminiscing about the best and worst of times of Fleet Street's 'Golden Years'. Such formidable women writers as Anne Scott James, Deirdre McSharry and Drusilla Beyfus remembered being hired for their first job by Harold, who championed their work in an industry then dominated by men. Deirdre McSharry described him as: '*Absolutely brilliant. I learned all that I know about lay-out and photography from him. He had an odd habit of putting any copy you left with him under the carpet.*'

Lord Snowdon valued Harold's creative spark, recognising his powers of alchemy, not dissimilar to his own. Appropriately for an editor described in his youth as '*bringing the razzamatazz of show business to Fleet Street*', Harold first noticed the talent of Anthony Armstrong-Jones, as he was then, when he saw the young photographer's giant, blown-up, black and white theatrical publicity photos displayed outside West End theatres.

As a long-time admirer of the US publications *Life* and *Look*, Harold was convinced British newspapers needed more such elements of American-style photo-reportage to capture readers' attention. Struck by the raw vitality of Armstrong-Jones' work, he decided these were the types of eye-catching photos Fleet Street should be publishing. Typically, he set straight off, on spec, to meet the photographer.

Harold Keeble came to see me at the studio. He was starting Photo News on the Daily Express and it was the first time that newspapers started using big theatre photographs to illustrate their theatre notices. He never filed photographs;

he'd just hide them under the edge of the carpet in his office where nobody else would find them.

In those days I used to go to Stratford [to the RSC theatre] *and drive back later that night after I'd photographed the play and found that if I printed them beautifully and dried them properly, quite often Keeble wouldn't use them because he didn't think they were hot news. On the other hand, if I didn't bother to finish them properly, but simply took them down to him wet, between two bits of blotting paper, at about two o'clock in the morning, he'd always use them even if it meant tearing out a whole page and redesigning it around the wet picture; he liked that kind of immediacy.*

I got tremendous excitement out of going down to Fleet Street with photographs and I got a huge kick out of seeing pictures I had taken appear the next day. I sometimes used to hang around Fleet Street until two o'clock in the morning to get the first copy off the presses.

The more I learnt about Harold's last weeks, and the immediate period following his death, the greater I saw was the esteem and love in which he was held by those closest to him.

One of his oldest friends, Lionel Green, phoned Gisela every evening for a year following Harold's death. In his own few remaining years, Lionel invited her to lunch whenever she came to London, an invitation that always included Vernon and their daughter Sonja.

Former journalists and editors who had worked with Harold, even on a relatively junior level, kept in touch with Gisela and Vernon for many years, often visiting the couple in Brighton to remember Harold and gossip about the old days.

Most of all, I was touched by Gisela's husband Vernon's feelings for Harold. Going right back to the late 1970s when Gisela first became involved with Harold, I remembered hearing that Vernon's respect and admiration for Harold knew no bounds – even in circumstances when other men might understandably have harboured very different feelings about the 'other man' in their wife's life.

The relationship between the Hendys and Harold was strikingly adult and civilised, founded on honesty, integrity and respect, far removed from messy games of subterfuge and emotional blackmail that can so often gnaw at the foundations of marriages and love affairs – before destroying them.

The secret to their harmonious coexistence seems to have been the openness of Gisela's relationship with Harold, which, far from being furtive and therefore prone to become the stuff of gossip, was openly recognised by Harold's colleagues and their close friends. Gisela had always been clear that her relationship with Harold did not become a threat to her marriage and the three continued to share an easy and happy relationship with each other.

Vernon therefore felt the loss of Harold keenly. Forty years later, his regard for Harold remains undiminished.

'*Your quest has revived memories of olden times*,' he emailed me when I first contacted him and Gisela out of the blue. '*What a different world Fleet Street was then. We just feel so privileged to have known him and had a glimpse into that world.*'

For Harold's sister in law Pat, as for Gisela and Vernon and the many former colleagues and friends who loved him, it is as if Harold is still among us. Perhaps he was right when, hearing about the death of his doctor who quietly slipped away in his sleep one night, he said that this is how the lucky ones go. Especially someone as young in mind and spirit as Harold, who refused ever to grow old.

If you are lucky, someone will enter your life at some point, often at a critical moment, most likely in your youth. They will sprinkle their magic over you, shake up your existence and eventually move on – sometimes far too soon. Sooner or later, often much later, you will recognise that you have changed. That's how it was with Harold, who walked into so many people's lives and transformed them. And we who remember hope to pass on what he taught us.

Because that's the thing with wizards. The magic never dies.

END

ACKNOWLEDGEMENTS

INEVITABLY, AFTER SEVERAL decades, memories of past events fade or become blurred, especially the names and official positions of people I worked with. I am grateful to the London College of Fashion for nudging my memory about the editors I first worked for at Vogue. Thanks also to fellow journalists Victor Olliver and Penny Rich and former PR executives Susi Jenkins, Astrid Sutton Sharkey, Vivienne Tomei-Robinson and Lyn Leigh, who all confirmed key names and dates. I am indebted to those friends who read my first draft and offered valuable advice and criticism. Thanks too to my eagle-eyed editor Lorna Read who cleaned up my manuscript and to tech 'wizard' Alan Officer, my website designer, who spent time experimenting with the appearance of the cover before I put out advance news of the publication online. Thank you also to Ken Dawson and Kate Coe at Creative Covers for steering me through the quicksand of the publication process and turning the book into a reality.

Special thanks to Harold Keeble's ex-colleagues Brian Freemantle, Christopher Ward and his former secretary Jacqueline Kidger for their recollections, also to Sir Allan Green, Nick Daubeny, and John 'Dak' Morton for retrieving magic moments. Most importantly, I could not have written this book without the support, encouragement and unique insights of Gisela and Vernon Hendy, who know more than anyone about Harold's personal background. Crucially, it was they who introduced me to his sister-in-law Pat Buchanan-Allen, who regaled me with recollections of his colourful, yet sometimes tragic, experiences. Sadly, Pat died before the publication of this book. I hope her son and grandchildren will enjoy reading about their extraordinary and brilliant relative.

About the Author

ALIX KIRSTA IS an investigative journalist specialising in crime and corruption, unsolved mysteries, psychology, and art world fraud on which she has written major features and cover stories for publications including *The Times*, *Sunday Times*, *Daily Telegraph*, *The Guardian*, *The Daily Mail.* She is the author of many non-fiction books including *Victims* and *Deadlier Than The Male,* and the best-selling *Stress Survival,* published in eighteen languages.

Printed in Great Britain
by Amazon

41209237R00139